Could Do Better

Love and Kisses
Carole
xox

Love Linda
xx
x

Love and Marmalade
Whizzer
xxx

Could Do Better

SCHOOL REPORTS OF THE
GREAT AND THE GOOD

Edited by
Catherine Hurley

POCKET
BOOKS

First published in Great Britain by Pocket Books, 2002
This edition published by Pocket Books, 2003
An imprint of Simon & Schuster UK Ltd
A Viacom Company

Introduction and selection © Catherine Hurley, 2002
Reports © see pages 159–62

5 7 9 10 8 6

Simon & Schuster UK Ltd
Africa House
64–78 Kingsway
London WC2B 6AH

www.simonsays.co.uk

Simon & Schuster Australia
Sydney

A CIP catalogue record for this book is available from the British Library

ISBN 0–7434–5025–6

Printed and bound by
Mackays of Chatham, Kent

Contents

Introduction   1

THE REPORTS

Entertainers   21

Michael Palin, Peter Cook, Sir Peter Ustinov, Eric Morecambe, Gary Morecambe, Alan Coren, Harry Enfield, Edward Enfield, Joan Collins, David Lean, Michael Winner, Dame Judi Dench, Dame Diana Rigg, Jane Asher, Richard Briers, John Lennon, Stephen Fry, Sir Norman Wisdom, Roy Hudd, Charlotte Church, Carol Vorderman, Nick Park, Pam Rhodes, Liz Barker, Simon Thomas, Woody Allen

Reporters   53

Lord Beaverbrook, Jeremy Paxman, Jeremy Hardy, Max Hastings, Richard Ingrams, Jon Snow, Alan Rusbridger, Sue Lawley, Sue MacGregor

Writers, Poets and Artists   67
  A. A. Milne, Augustus John, P. G. Wodehouse, Rupert Brooke,
  Siegfried Sassoon, Cyril Connolly, Cecil Beaton, Graham Greene,
  Philip Larkin, Dennis Potter, Richard Hoggart, Bruce Chatwin,
  Tom Paulin, Margaret Forster, Beryl Bainbridge, Jilly Cooper,
  Helen Fielding, Ken Follett, Hunter Davies, Philip Pullman,
  Howard Marks, Robert Graves

Statesmen and Women   95
  Herbert H. Asquith, Sir Winston Churchill, Clement Attlee, Sir Alec
  Douglas-Home, Sir Stafford Cripps, Sir Anthony Eden, Lady
  Margaret Thatcher, John Maynard Keynes, Lord Longford, Franklin
  D. Roosevelt, Eleanor Roosevelt, Dwight D. Eisenhower, John F.
  Kennedy, Jimmy Carter, George Bush, Ian Macfadyen, Arthur M.
  Schlesinger Jr, Viscount Montgomery of Alamein, Lord Louis
  Mountbatten, Lord Michael Heseltine, Michael Foot, Lord Ashdown,
  John Redwood, Lord David Owen, Lord David Steel

Inventors, Explorers, Innovators and Other Movers
  and Shakers   129
  John Polyani, Paul Nurse, Sir Ranulph Fiennes, Dame Stella
  Rimington, J. Edgar Hoover, Diana, Princess of Wales, Duchess of
  Windsor, Carl Gustav Jung, Isaiah Berlin, A. J. Ayer, John Arlott,
  Richard Dunwoody

In Fiction   143
The Last Word   153

Acknowledgements   157
Sources   159

Introduction

Among the many entertaining replies to my request for copies of school reports was this one from Neil Kinnock: 'I have no surviving copies of my reports because I destroyed them before my parents could see them. The excuses that I gave at the end of each term for about six years were major pieces of inventiveness. I went to the Lewis School, Pengam in Wales ... and my reports ... were truly and consistently appalling.' Auberon Waugh wrote about adopting a similar tactic, intercepting the post during holidays from Downside, steaming open anything from the school and extracting any reports that were 'outrageously offensive'.

While not everyone would have taken such drastic action, it became clear as I put together this collection that, however significant the reports might have seemed at the time, keeping track of them over the course of a lifetime – like, say, a birth certificate or a graduation photo – was not exactly common practice. It would seem that unless a family is inclined to be its own archivist, a school report, once received, digested, smarted over or crowed about, is of no further practical value to its recipient. After all, it's not as if you'll be asked to present it at a job interview.

Nonetheless and thankfully for this book, a good number of eminent people (or more probably their mothers and sometimes fathers) have kept their school reports. Sometimes very consciously, like the bound volumes of Jane Asher's and Jon Snow's, or tucked away in a parent's drawer like Jeremy Paxman's, whose mother posted his to him with a note saying, 'If only you had worked hard all the time, you might have done a lot better.'

It has been a pleasure to receive and read these fragments of personal history and I like to think that, in the main, the contributors have enjoyed this quick Proustian reminder of their adolescent selves.

> As we read the school reports on our children, we realize a sense of relief that can rise to delight that – thank Heaven – nobody is reporting in this fashion on us.
>
> J. B. Priestley

The very thought of a school report can transport us straight back to the first time we suffered critical judgement and were assessed by the disinterested world outside our families. In a culture as obsessed with education as ours, it's not surprising that such weight should be attached to these first pointers to our success, or otherwise. So for every one respondent who happily remembered their school days, there were at least twice as many who made it clear they'd firmly closed the door on the whole thing. And even if our memories are good ones, we should beware of the rose-tinted spectacles effect. A common experience among the friends who shared their reports with me was the shock of discovering that they were by no means as exceptional as they'd remembered.

Regarding history's high achievers, I have relied upon the work of biographers whose sections on their subjects' schooldays often include illuminating passages from their reports. Sometimes, as in the case of Woody Allen or Michael Heseltine, I've slightly bent the rules about what exactly constitutes a report – but only when I couldn't resist the material.

Many people who had long since lost track of their reports gave their permission for me to contact their old schools. When I first set about this project I assumed that the older schools especially would at least have copies of reports of their more illustrious alumni. But with schools as with individuals, the significance of their report writing is not reflected in whether they have kept them or not. The Second World War played havoc with schools' record-keeping, as illustrated by June Whitfield's reply to my request for her reports: 'My schooling was during the war, and my schools kept evacuating themselves, I doubt there are any records of my education!' Of course, anecdotes about celebrated or notorious reports have been handed down through the years and regularly feature in Heads' after-dinner speeches – some of these oral histories have made it into the book. But although I have had many fruitful conversations with teachers and headmasters about reports and the actual writing of them, there were, alas, no handy archives to which I could refer and plunder.

This may change with the advent of computerized reports and less cumbersome methods of storage. But some would argue that this same technology makes retaining them as any sort of historical or social record less necessary. There's no doubt that reports from thirty or more years ago make much more interesting reading than present-day examples, and this isn't only due to hindsight; there is an obvious piquancy in discovering that Nobel prize winner, John Polanyi, didn't look as if he'd amount to very much at the age of sixteen. As Steve Burgoyne, the present Headmaster of Sexey's School in Somerset replied to my enquiry about Ned Sherrin: 'I'm sure that reports were highly distinctive and individual in Mr Sherrin's day, but I'm sorry to say that, in the litigious twenty-first century, we have to be very careful what we write, so reports tend to be very earnest, comprehensive documents.' Any parent of a school-age child will concur with the 'earnestness' tag, but perhaps after reading some of the less-than-earnest reports here, they might be grateful for that restraint. Sometimes the brutality of the language used seems almost to emulate the corporal punishment for which English public schools were once renowned.

More common than outright cruelty, certainly in the English school report, was sarcasm. It may be dismissed as the lowest form of wit, although not by the man who wrote to the *Daily Telegraph* (during one of their occasional flurries of letters about schooldays) to take issue with a Northampton Head's edict against the use of sarcasm in school reports. This threatened 'one of the great art forms of British life' according to the correspondent, citing a treasured memory from Haileybury of the term a pupil skipped general studies every single week and received the remark 'Consistent' on his report.

Whether or not the likes of 'Exam result: 4%. Effortlessly achieved' constitutes an art form, it's certainly very British, and may be usefully compared with reports from elsewhere – such as those of an American boy who applied to transfer to an English public school. Sifting through his reports to try and get the boy's measure, the Headmaster gave up after coming across the comment: 'Gee Aaron, you were great!'

It's a wonder that more victims of verbal abuse didn't adopt the Kinnock/Waugh tactic. Or, indeed, Augustus John's reaction, which was to punch an offending master. But by and large, we can only guess at what effect these reports had upon their recipients. Looking down at them from the pinnacle of success that many of the contributors have achieved must be gratifying, but how must it have felt to have been told, like A. J. 'Freddie' Ayer, that the trouble with him was that he didn't know when he wasn't wanted? Luckily, some more significant reactions have been recorded for posterity so, for example, we know that but for A. A. Milne's bad mathematics report, Winnie the Pooh and Christopher Robin might never have been born.

A framed copy of this hangs in the halls of The Perse, Cambridge.

And what of the parents? Well into the second half of the twentieth century, it's quite likely that the head of the household's reaction to a report would have been similar to that of Augustus John's father who, following a string of reports of Gussie's bad behaviour, 'had recourse to the old-fashioned punishment of caning'. Or A. A. Milne's father who, despite its patent inaccuracy, took as gospel the poor report of his son's results in Maths. If a teacher decreed that you were 'bad', 'untidy', 'dirty', 'pleased with yourself', 'lazy', or, indeed, 'clever', then so you were – no questions asked. That attitudes were changing in the 1960s may perhaps be gauged from the King's School, Ely, mother who, going over her son's unprepossessing report with his teacher, volunteered: 'I know he's not very exciting at school, but he's a big dear at home.'

I hope this collection will give an impression of how reports have developed over the 150 years or so from the earliest here (H. H. Asquith's in the 1860s) to Charlotte Church's report from 2001. Not only has the form of the report changed enormously over the years – from its first appearance as a letter from the Tutor to the parents, to today's computerized 'tick' box with varying amounts of individual comment – its role in the educational process has also changed. While the formal end-of-term system of reporting gradually became commonplace throughout both the private and state sectors, it is also evident that, in recent years, a fundamental shift of emphasis has taken place.

Ian Thorpe, Deputy Head of Manchester Grammar, describes the change during his teaching career as moving from looking back, to one of target-setting, with the emphasis being on how the pupil should respond. This process is reinforced by the practice of discussing the report with the pupil before releasing it to the parents. This suggests that where once the role of the report was to record how a child had fared in a given institution, it is now also intended as a record of how well the institution has done by the child.

Some of these changes can be traced back to the increase in parents' active involvement in their children's education, via consultation evenings. Turning this involvement into a formal arrangement was not always enthusiastically embraced (then as now, one imagines). As recently as the 1970s, in one boarding school house, the suggestion of a parent–teacher meeting over a buffet lunch to discuss the progress of individual pupils was greeted with horror as a practically Leninist innovation (or 'progressive', as described in another public school). But once parental involvement became an accepted part of school life, the report became the central means for teacher–parent communication. And the knowledge that one would probably be called upon to defend any comment on a child's progress, face-to-face with a parent, has doubtless led many teachers to a restraint that is not evident in reports from the early part of the twentieth century.

As the function of the school report changed, so has the whole process of 'writing' them. According to Ian Matheson, retired Second Master at the King's School, Ely, at the beginning of his thirty-five year teaching career reports were all written collectively, in one room, with sometimes a bottle of sherry to ease the burden. The younger teachers would have been able to benefit from their more experienced colleagues (although perhaps not going as far as the apocryphal master who leaned over to a colleague scribbling reports beside him to say, 'tell me, how does one spell bastard?')

In *Eton – How it Works* (Faber, 1967) James D. R. McConnell outlined accepted procedure for report-writing which is still largely followed there today as the following example of an Eton report shows:

Dear _____

I hope that _____ did not look too pale and weary on his return to you this week. Fortunately, the Trials results brought something of a glow to his cheeks, quite deservedly, and I hope that he is now aiming for nothing less than straight A grades at GCSE. He will be very pleased with his German, where he has been rewarded during the half with seven show-ups, and an excellent report too. Similarly, his Maths has come up trumps, which is not quite the same as his English, where he does not yet hold a winning hand. He is up to one of the best English teachers in the school, so he should be taking advantage of this, rather than trying to cut corners as he has done on one or two occasions. His French is drifting a bit: I have some sympathies with a less than vigorous approach, as the play we are studying is excruciatingly dull, and the grammar all looks just familiar enough to the boys for them to think they know it. But he is a good linguist, and could well contemplate something in the language line for his A levels. His Music teacher fires off a timely warning about his relying too much on the computer (in this case for his composition). _____ has certainly been better this half in controlling the non-academic use of his laptop, but it is still a draw for many of his adoring fans, who lounge on his 'double bed' (now declared a fire risk by a pernickety fire officer on inspection of the house last week), hunting and destroying the enemy, or whatever it is you do with these things.

. . . Mangoes, it seems may not be the only fruit. All quiet at the moment. I await the next course with interest. Even if nothing comes of it, the creative energy and spurts of enthusiasm are to be encouraged. Musically, I think we may have something of a minor success over the supervision of the quartet, in that the Director of Music was very sympathetic. I am sorry that I only heard the first section of the Bach Chaconne when ____ played it (beautifully) in Prayers last Monday. He was much more confident too than on his last appearance before the house. I gather he is now on to a piece of diabolic complexity. What a range of music he has played in public this half, from Bach to Ysaye, via Dvorak.

I realize with some embarrassment that I have been rather neglectful of ____'s fitness this half. This has not been wilful neglect, just ineffi-ciency on my part. I have made a note to take this in hand in January. However, his fitness levels will be topped up on a daily (and nightly) basis here, with the miles he travels around the house. The business-like figure of a dressing-gowned ____ beetling along a corridor at night 'just off to ask Jeremy something, Sir' or 'just looking for some toothpaste' (what do they do with the stuff? The house is full of nocturnal prowlers on the lookout for stray tubes of toothpaste.)

This report exhibits a level of individual attention and pastoral care that many parents would feel is missing in their children's school life today. And it is surely this which is really being expressed in debates over the handwritten versus the computerized report – the argument being that technology is changing their very nature, with the handwrit-ten report seen to symbolize an individual approach to education, and the computer its demise.

However, in research conducted by Power and Clark (*The Right to Know: Parents, School Reports and Parents' Evenings*) strong feelings were often recorded *against* hand written reports. This was sometimes along the lines of 'The handwriting was absolutely disgusting', but a greater antipathy was expressed towards the generalized nature of comments, and the feeling that the report could have been written about any child. So while one may learn something of the character of the teacher writing the report through the handwriting, it would be wrong to conclude that a handwritten report is necessarily a more individual one: 'Steady Progress', which crops up in report after report from Eton to Harrow, Downside to Uppingham, remains resolutely opaque, however copperplate the script. There is the notorious story of the teacher writing of a pupil who clearly hadn't made a great impression: 'He has attended his lessons.' As the report travelled up the school hierarchy, it was pointed out to the teacher that in fact the pupil had been exempt from these lessons. His solution was simply to insert a handwritten 'not' before 'attended'.

A handwritten report is not necessarily a more personal one . . .

The problem is not, of course, the form of the report, but rather the content. And one of the more dubious influences brought about through technology is the widespread use of 'statement banks' in report writing. The thought that it is a mere click of 'BX26' (as it is known to a primary school teacher of my acquaintance) that is being used to assess your child surely must contribute to parents' anxiety about over-generalized reports.

In an endeavour to maintain the personal touch, in 2000 Putney Girls' School experimented with a speech-to-text service in which teachers spoke their reports down the phone to a transcription service. According to Deputy Head Margaret Chandler, this 'Reports by Phone' experiment was largely welcomed by teachers and parents alike. The system let them down, however, as the transcription service was unable to keep up with the volume of reports generated or to meet the required standard of syntax and spelling; the transcribers fell down on practice/practise and other spelling errors which caused them to fall foul of Putney's teachers. Essentially, the school's idea was ahead of the technology available.

From an educational professional's point of view, the case can be made that the standard of school reporting has actually improved. Ian Thorpe at Manchester Grammar argues that their reports system (a mixture of the 'tick box' form and written comment) suits both the teachers who have to write them, and the parents and their children. He thinks that this system helps to ensure a uniform standard, and makes it easier to store the reports (clearly a problem in long-established schools) – and therefore easier to refer back and build up an evolving picture of the child, as well as providing more of an opportunity to spot mistakes (i.e. fewer English reports where a child's spelling is criticized as 'appaling').

But I'm not so sure: where in the statement bank might the ringing non-endorsement 'he must not make a pose of being sardonic' (Nottingham High School, 1963) appear? Mr Matheson at the King's School prided himself on a smart turn of phrase and certainly, in some of the older reports, the way language is used comes as a delight to the jargon-corroded reader. As a parent, I think I'd rather be told the truth elegantly (however unpalatable).

However the writing and the content of school reports may have changed, teachers' attitudes have stayed much the same over the years. Some hate the whole process, some relish it – although I suspect that there's much less of the latter these days. The other overriding problem, and something that can't have changed at all, is that teachers are almost always presented with a class where one or two will stand out at either end of the spectrum, but most are in a big, average group in the middle. And what do you say about them? A quick click of 'BX26' is today's teacher's solution, whereas in the past there were more options available. Like the teacher who, confronted with a boy of lacklustre academic ability and desperate for something positive to sum him up, described how the boy had discovered the teacher's dog lying injured in

13

the road and had brought it home. Memorably irrelevant on one level, but on another and arguably more important one, memorably illuminating.

Which brings us back to the whole significance of school reports, in the wider context of later life and career. If the majority of us occupy that middle band, neither very good nor very bad, do they have any value as signposts to the future? Parents take heart from this description: at the age of seven, of he who later 'held senates enchained by his eloquence and audiences by his wit, was, by common consent of both parent and preceptor, pronounced to be "a most impenetrable dunce!" (from Moore's *Life of Sheridan*). The joy in reading many of the reports in this collection is discovering those that are spectacularly wrong as well as those that are spectacularly right. The best way of showing this gap (or otherwise) between early assessment and final destination is by the profession for which these people became best known, and so that is how the reports are presented here.

It should, however, be borne in mind that life beyond school is seldom as straightforward and clear-cut as Cyril Morgan Brown, Headmaster at St Edmund's School, Hindhead, made out when he wrote of one boy who had misspelt the Latin *misit* as *missit*: 'A boy who does that will never make anything of his life.'

EXAMS AND
· REPORTS ·

BRIGHTENING SCHOOL REPORTS
[1925]

It is my intention to go down to history as the man who revolutionised report-writing in schools.'

There are roughly four styles now in vogue:

1. The Horticultural style – 'Coming on nicely' or 'Maturing well;'

2. The Puppy-training style – 'Intelligent: he responds well to correction;'

3. The Blunt style – 'He is a horrid little boy and I hate him.' after which one writes 'BUT' and makes an arrow pointing to the place where it says *The holidays begin on July 27th*;' and

4. The up-to-date Psycho-analytical style which is not much encouraged but which runs something like this:

'His listlessness is a natural protective armour against brain-fag; obviously suffering from serious neuroses; unless he goes to Madeira for a month's complete change and rest he will certainly become insane.'

5. The Illegible style.

May I tell you a little story?

There was once a headmaster who, after reading a boy's report, wrote at the bottom of it, 'Let him take heed to his pincushions.'

That, at any rate is what the boy's father made of it; so he wrote to the headmaster, who replied, 'I am indeed sorry. I wrote not "pincushions" but "pincushions."'

The word, of course, was 'penmanship'; the masters had all complained of the boy's handwriting, and the Head wrote, 'Let him take heed to his penmanship.'

This is the scheme which I propose: when the end of the term comes I am going to have the points of the mental compass printed at the top of each report; the North will represent Genius: the West, Pious Endeavour; between the two there will be a Magnetic North, which of course will represent myself: there will be correspondingly a Phlegmatic South. And so on. It will look like this:

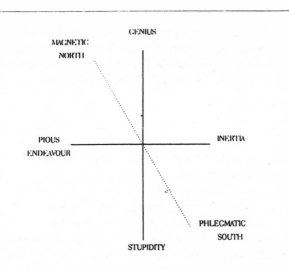

Then all I shall have to write will be something of this sort:

Hawtrey III. Keeps a steady southwesterly course.

Jones. Last seen heading for the Phlegmatic South. Reported becalmed.

Robinson. Still endeavouring to find a N.E. Passage.

Bloggins. Believed, after a rough passage, to have discovered the South Pole.

The Reports

In a letter to the *Telegraph*, the writer, politician and historian Sir Robert Rhodes James noted his debt to a master who'd written about him, aged thirteen: 'He has the makings of a serious historian.' This was the beginning of his ambition, the more noteworthy because it came from a master feared by both boys and parents during Rhodes James' time at Sedbergh. Wrote Rhodes James of his own report: 'This is an example of how a good teacher can use reports to encourage and inspire as well as to give scathing – and accurate – character analyses.' Or, perhaps not so accurate?

Entertainers

I remember being called into the headmaster's study once to account for my general recalcitrance. The Sausage, as we called him, said to me, 'You really are a very strange boy, Parsons. I wonder what you intend to do with your life.'

With all the confidence of youth, and not a little asperity, I replied, 'I want to leave this place with all its untalented people as soon as possible and become an actor.'

He laughed. If you are reading this now, Sausage, I wonder if you are still laughing.

from *I, An Actor* by Nicholas Craig

Michael Palin (1943–)

Writer and comedian, co-creator of *Monty Python*

SHREWSBURY SCHOOL, SHROPSHIRE, 1960

Housemaster's final report	*There are doubts beginning to creep in here which have been noticeably absent from his work reports of the past. I very much hope this is a passing phase. Mr Brown tells me that it appears he has easily passed in Geography – a very commendable effort in so short a time. There may be a vestige of truth in Mr Charlesworth's last remark. I too have noticed symptoms of the same sort of thing, a slightly put-on manner of affectation, perhaps a sort of aftermath of his fine performance in the School Play. We're all for a bit of jollity and mild eye-flashing business, but he must not try to get away altogether with this slightly facile manner.* *He has the makings of a splendid person. Let him ensure that his foundations are thoroughly sound.*
Headmaster's comments	*I think he is just a teeny bit pleased with himself – or so I am prepared to hazard.*

Peter Cook (1937–1995)

Comedian, satirist

ST BEDE'S, EASTBOURNE 1945–51 AND RADLEY COLLEGE, ABINGDON 1951–56

St Bede's, final report	*Originality of thought and a command of words give him a maturity of style beyond his years. In speech or essay he is never dull and his work should always be interesting.*
Radley, 1953, Warden's report	*There can be no doubt about Peter's ability but I am disappointed that he does not make more positive use of it. I recall literary and artistic talent which he seems content to let sleep, doing in the classroom no more than is required of him and making little effort to find outside avenues of fulfilment. There are faint signs already that it may lead to a most undesirable cynicism of outlook.*
Final report	*An unruffled temperament who has had considerable influence, especially in his own cultural field. He has qualities, not least a certain elusiveness – which should render him a most useful member of the Foreign Service.*

Sir Peter Ustinov CBE (1921–)

Actor, director, playwright, novelist

MR GIBBS' PREPARATORY SCHOOL, LONDON 1927–1934
AND WESTMINSTER SCHOOL

Headmaster's report	*We know that he has unusual ability and his slowness in the more 'cut and dried' subjects, e.g. L. Gram., only emphasizes his brilliance in more original work. He has a gentle and charming nature and I shall always value the fine example he has set in the school during his time here.*
Westminster	*He shows great originality, which must be curbed at all costs.*

Eric Morecambe OBE (1926–84)

(John Eric Bartholomew)

Comedian, one half of Morecambe and Wise

LANCASTER ROAD JUNIOR SCHOOL

Headmaster	*This boy will never get anywhere in life.*

Like father, like son?

Gary Morecambe

(son of Eric)

HARDENWICK SCHOOL, HERTS, 1966

English master	*A charming boy, who makes no effort whatsoever and whose main aim in life appears to be the disposing of work in the minimum time possible.*
Headmaster	*. . . If he cannot make the effort himself we shall have to adopt firmer tactics.*

Alan Coren (1938–)

Journalist and broadcaster

EAST BARNET GRAMMAR SCHOOL

Physics	*Coren's grasp of elementary dynamics is truly astonishing. Had he lived in an earlier eon, I have little doubt but that the wheel would now be square and the principle of the lever just one more of man's impossible dreams.*

Harry Enfield (1961–)

Comedian

ARUNDALE SCHOOL AND DORSET HOUSE, SUSSEX,
1965–70

Harry Enfield's reports remark mostly upon his 'liveliness', a word which, like 'easygoing', has a uniquely negative connotation when used in a school report.

1965, aged 6½	*Very talkative. Unfortunately what he has to say is not always relevant.*
Art	*Fair, talks too much.*
Aged 8, Headmaster	*His reputation and liveliness has outpaced him.*
Aged 11, Headmaster	*Perhaps his science will become more scientific next term.* *. . . rarely starved for an opinion on any topic.*
Physics	*An excellent start, although he could think a little longer before asking questions. Incidentally, he has the makings of a first rate public speaker.*

Harry's 'liveliness' extended to that most important barometer of a schoolboy's worth – games.

Cricket	*He doesn't really hit the ball hard enough but he calls his partners to run with such conviction that one would believe that the ball was speeding away . . . his conversation keeps his side amused and his efforts to avoid having to field are ingenious. He is a cheerful chap but no cricketer.*
Rugby	*Sometimes I think he is just a spectator who has strayed. This is not his game, but he bore it nobly.*

Edward Enfield (1929–)

Journalist

ASHBURY COLLEGE, CANADA, 1940–44 AND
WESTMINISTER SCHOOL, 1944–48

Less 'lively' than his son, Harry. Just as 'lively' is bad in the language of school reports, 'plodder' hasn't the pejorative connotations that we would read into it today. It is to be understood in the Aesopian sense, i.e. like the turtle, a 'plodder' will come through in the end.

Ashbury College	Football: *A reliable, though slow, and as yet light, fullback.*
Westminster School	Latin: *A plodder.*

Joan Collins OBE (1933–)

Actress, producer, novelist

RADA, c. 1945

On leaving	With so much in her favour the student is hampered by the weakness of her voice. She seems to lack the confidence to project and make the most of the voice she does possess. If she will make up her mind to cast away fear, doubt and self-consciousness, she will find her confidence increasing, and the unsure element in her acting will disappear. Otherwise it will be 'the films' for her, and that would be such a pity!

David Lean (1908–1991)

Director of film classics such as *Brief Encounter*, *Lawrence of Arabia*

LEIGHTON PARK SCHOOL, READING, 1922–25

From a letter to the Headmaster of Leighton Park from Major Atkinson, Head of The Limes, which David was leaving:

The boy has been with me for some time and I have found him to be keen, honest and extremely hardworking. However, two terms ago I was of the opinion that he never would be suitable for public school life owing to the fact that he did not appear to make any progress in his work, and therefore I advised his father to give him an outdoor life. Since then he has made very rapid progress and appears to have turned the corner (I say this in spite of the marks obtained). He is by no means at his best during examinations, but I can honestly say I shall be very sorry when he leaves me as I have found he is liked by every master and boy in the school. Finally, I can only add that it is my firm opinion that he will be a credit to any school.

Despite his lack of academic success, Leighton Park agreed.

First report	*[he has] an interest which should help him in all departments of school life . . . cheerful, even when he grouses . . . lacks the will to work at distasteful subjects.*
July 1923	*He is greatly to be congratulated on his help . . . Full of ideas both in a Form Social and in a House Social. In his work he repays personal attention – often finds it difficult to progress without it.*

By the following year, he was showing . . .

	. . . encouraging improvement . . . executive and masterful, almost too domineering! . . . He has been of a very great help to his Form and his Form master.
1925, aged 17 and now a House Prefect	*A boy of courage and we admire him for it.*

Michael Winner (1935–)

Director, actor

ST CHRISTOPHER'S SCHOOL, LETCHWORTH, 1940s

1942, aged 6 years, 4 months	*Michael has suddenly become a very noisy person and rather fancies himself as a humorist. This is sometimes disturbing in group activities such as singing. He is a very lively and constructive member of the group.*
1942, aged 6 years, 11 months	*His most popular asset is his love of story-telling, he does this chiefly at dinner time and there is a great demand to sit at his table. Michael has not yet learnt to work quietly and this can be very tiring.*
1943, aged 7	*Michael has a great sense of fairness, not only where he himself is concerned. He spontaneously interferes on behalf of any child whom he thinks is not able to stand up for itself. He is much respected and listened to by the other children in consequence.*

1946, aged 10	*Michael is more considerate and reasonable but alas! If there is anything to be done he is generally missing.*
1947, aged 12	*Michael's progress of last term has not been maintained. He is cocksure and is it really a defence? He has the reputation of being movie mad and should try to take up some more creative hobby.*

Dame Judi Dench OBE (1934–)

Actress

THE MOUNT SCHOOL, YORK

Headmaster	*Judi would be a very good pupil if she lived in this world.*

Dame Diana Rigg CBE (1938–)

Actress

ST CHRISTOPHER'S, LITTLE MISSENDEN, c.1946

Matron's report	*Diana has been very tiresome in the dormitory this term.*

Jane Asher (1946–)

Actress, novelist, businesswoman

MISS LAMBERT'S PNEU, LONDON, 1956–1961

The pattern for stellar reports was set early. It seems that she was going to be a success at whatever – acting or cake-making – she set her mind to.

Nursery, aged 3 years, 5 months	*Jane has spent a very successful first term in the nursery. She is extremely capable, self possessed, and intelligent for her age. Her speech is very advanced, and she talks a great deal. She has a strong character and knows exactly what she wants to do. She sometimes wants another child's piece of apparatus and is most upset when she cannot have it. She is always very reasonable however when it is explained to her that the nursery toys have to be shared.*
	She likes the other children and is extremely popular with them, especially with Peter's friends. She is very affectionate and is always delighted to see Peter at garden time.
	Jane enjoys painting very much and has a passion for green paint, she is also interested in stories and makes unusually intelligent comments. She joins in the Singing Games with enthusiasm.
	In the garden she likes to play on the swingboat most of all. Another favourite occupation this term has been 'tea parties' using water for the tea.

Miss Lambert's PNEU, London	*Her zestful approach to everything, in lessons and out, is charming. She is helpful and courteous, and sensible and good tempered when her exuberance is checked.*

Though there was *some* cause for concern:

Writing	*Very neat and legible. She should check a very slight tendency for it occasionally to lean backwards.*

or

She must guard against a slight tendency to carelessness, which is starting to appear, probably through overconfidence . . . Her conduct has been very good, she is unselfish and most co-operative though sometimes she acts a little thoughtlessly

Richard Briers (1934–)

Actor

ROKEBY SCHOOL, WIMBLEDON

Headmaster's report	*It would seem that Briers thinks he is running the school and not me. If this attitude persists one of us will have to leave.*

John Lennon (1940–1980)

Musician

QUARRY BANK SCHOOL, LIVERPOOL, 1957

Lennon was a bright boy who seemed not to see the point of school. His reports reflected this:

> *Certainly on the road to failure . . . hopeless . . . rather a clown in class . . . wasting other pupils' time.*

But all hope was not lost:

July 1957 (on leaving)	*He has been a trouble spot for many years in discipline, but has somewhat mended his ways. Requires the sanction of 'losing a job' to keep him on the rails. But I believe he is not beyond redemption and he could really turn out a fairly responsible adult who might go far.*

Stephen Fry (1957–)

Comedian, playwright, novelist

UPPINGHAM SCHOOL, RUTLAND, 1970–72

Headmaster's report	*He has glaring faults and they have certainly glared at us this term.*
1971	*I have nothing more to say.*
1972	English: *Bottom, rightly.*
Headmaster's report	*Not a happy figure, I fear. However, so long as Mr. Frowde is prepared to soldier on, I am.*

Alas, he wasn't. Fry was expelled from Uppingham in 1972.

Sir Norman Wisdom OBE (1915–)

Actor

Last report from Army Education Course exam	*The boy is every inch a fool but luckily for him he's not very tall.*
	Although I doubt any possibility of his ever being promoted, he may get sufficient marks to obtain his proficiency pay, and who knows, with a little bit of luck, he may perhaps, in time – about twenty-one years – get a pension.

Roy Hudd (1936–)

Entertainer

CROYDON SECONDARY TECHNICAL SCHOOL

> *This boy has a rag-bag mind stuffed with information of no possible interest to anyone but himself.*

Charlotte Church (1986–)

Singer

HOWELL'S SCHOOL, LLANDAFF, 2001

Absences: 85   Lates: 6

July 2001	*Charlotte has achieved some excellent results in these examinations and it is a sign of her commitment to do well. It is not easy to juggle her academic studies with a successful career. I think she has enjoyed being able to be in a class situation for a time.*
	Music: *I am delighted with Charlotte's result; despite her absence she has been able to catch up on the work missed and gained a very good examination mark. Charlotte is always keen, conscientious and participates well in class. It was indeed a pleasure to hear her sing 'Can't Help Lovin' Dat Man of Mine' for her individual performance. It was superb performance. I look forward very much to hearing it on the new CD . . .*

Carol Vorderman (1960–)

TV Presenter, *Countdown*

YSGOL MAIR J. M. & I., RHYL, 1969

Achieving 586 out of a total of 600 marks in the various subjects, the class teacher had this to say about the *Countdown* presenter-to-be:

Aged 8	*An excellent result in every way. Carol has a masterly hold over mathematical computation which should prove profitable later on. She is a very helpful and conscientious girl.*

Nick Park (1958–)

Founder of Aardman Animation and creator of Wallace & Gromit

ST TERESA'S R.C. PRIMARY, PRESTON, LANCS, 1963 AND
ST OSWALD'S PRIMARY, LONGTON

St Teresa's	*Nicholas is inclined to be lazy. He is an artistic child and produces beautiful drawings and writing.*
St Oswald's Primary	*Inclined to dream. Could do better if he tried.*

Pam Rhodes (1950–)

Presenter, *Songs of Praise*

GOSPORT COUNTY GRAMMAR SCHOOL, 1967

Sixth Form general report	*With infectious enthusiasm Pamela contributes fully to the corporate life of the school. Although unassuming and modest, she has the ability to lead and organise others; her attitude to her work is equally praiseworthy. She sets high standards for herself and others.*

Which is about the tenor of most of her reports, most prescient being her leaving report from the Highbury Technical College, Intensive Secretarial course from which she graduated in 1969:

A charming personality with dramatic leaning, she will do well in a secretarial position which offers her scope for dramatic flair.

Liz Barker (1975–)

Presenter, *Blue Peter*

IMPINGTON VILLAGE COLLEGE, CAMBRIDGE,

Record of achievement	*Her practical skills have improved a great deal as she becomes more confident, particularly in Science. Her investigation on 'Cleanliness' on the 'Keeping Clean' topic showed good group skills . . .*
	She is a creative student who has produced work in art which reflects her imagination and obvious enjoyment.

Simon Thomas (1972–)

Presenter, *Blue Peter*

ST JOHN'S SCHOOL, LEATHERHEAD

Housemaster's report, Christmas 1987	*The more I see of Simon the more impressed I am. He has clearly put in a great deal of effort this term and it has paid dividends – the only real complaint is that he is too quiet but I'm sure he will strive to overcome this.*
Summer 1991	History: *He was never at his best in the sixteenth century but worked conscientiously and presented his essays well.*
Housemaster's report	*I could not have wished for a better House Captain than Simon – he has been a tower of strength, running the House very efficiently, taking the initiative when the need arose and giving a strong lead all the time.*

Woody Allen (1935–)

(Allen Stewart Konigsberg)

Director, actor, comedian, musician

NEW YORK UNIVERSITY

Reviewing board at NYU at the end of his first semester:

> *While cautiously holding out some hope of readmission suggested he seek counselling for his inability to take life seriously.*

Reporters

Journalism is the only job that requires no degrees, no diplomas and no specialized knowledge of any kind.

Patrick Campbell, *My Life & Easy Times*

Lord Beaverbrook (1879–1964)

(William Maxwell Aitken)

Newspaper magnate, proprietor of the *Daily Express*, politician

HARKINS ACADEMY, NEW BRUNSWICK, CANADA

Headmaster's report, on leaving	*I never believed that he would be in any way successful. This was simply because he never stuck at anything but was switching from one idea to another. There was never any doubt about his ability but he was so mischievous that I did not believe his ability would ever possibly carry him to success.*

Jeremy Paxman (1950–)

Journalist, *Newsnight* presenter, writer

MALVERN COLLEGE, 1962–68

Housemaster's report	*He has improved this term, and has made valuable contributions. His stubbornness is in his nature, and could be an asset when directed to sound ends. But his flying off the handle will only mar his efforts, and he must learn tact while not losing his outspokenness.*
English report	*His essays continue to suffer from ingrained grammatical faults, particularly in punctuation, but what is really at fault is his whole approach to his work. It is a pity that the threat of failure in his exams has not helped him to grow out of a tediously lackadaisical uncooperativeness.*

Jeremy Hardy (1961–)

Journalist, broadcaster, comedian

FARNHAM COLLEGE, 1976

Drama	*An excellent year's work both in productions and class – although Jeremy must be prepared to be serious sometimes!*
Form tutor	*It is clear from Jeremy's report that while he is intelligent and capable of a high standard of work, his general zest for life does not always allow him to do justice to himself. He does not have, as yet, sufficient of that particular aspect of maturity which understands that there are in life many things which have to be done which are boring and/or unpleasant and even those things which are mostly pleasant have their boring parts too. He is beginning to understand it, but he hasn't yet fully got there and accepted it.*
Year tutor	*I have been disappointed by Jeremy's synthetic mood this year. With so much potential talent and vitality, he ought to be a leader not a sideliner.*

Sir Max Hastings (1945–)

Newspaper editor, *Daily Telegraph* and *Evening Standard*, military historian

CHARTERHOUSE, 1959–63

Housemaster's report	*I will not quite say, as someone once said of Kipling, that all the good fairies came to his christening and they were all drunk, but certainly many came and they were none of them quite sober . . . Everyone likes him, but no one knows from day to day what he may do next . . . His present goal seems to be a tub in Hyde Park.*
English Literature	*When in his dogmatic moods he writes appalling essays, devoid of all argument, of a sort that will catch the examiner's eye all right but will certainly antagonize him.*
Maths	*He gradually found his way to the bottom then raised himself at the very end, perhaps through his rival's illness. He finds the subject difficult but should not make this an excuse for idleness.*

French	*He plummeted to the bottom of the Form in the first fortnight. It is a position which ill becomes a scholar, and we have looked for signs of surfacing; but there he is still, and only the bubbles rise.*
Scripture	*Appears to have some intelligence, but to think that this subject is not worth the exercise of it.*

Richard Ingrams (1937–)

Founder-editor, *Private Eye* and *The Oldie*

SHREWSBURY SCHOOL

In his first year, his Housemaster reported him:

> *silent . . . sober . . . still a child in many ways.*

And then, the year his father died suddenly and Ingrams' academic work suffered, his Form master wrote that he was:

> *downright careless*

and his Greek master put it:

> *It is hard to tell if the outward attitude of – to say the least – indifference to his work is just an attitude or not. He has too much ability, surely to play at cynicism.*

Then, still later:

Housemaster	*He is in the process of emerging from his shell, and there will be a certain amount of diversionary activity, some of it probably ill-judged, but I do not doubt that the outcome in the long run will be good, for he has a core of solid good sense.*
	At times last year I felt he was behaving a little out of character – emulating his brother, perhaps, as a 'figure'. This term he seems more natural, more himself – and on the whole the better for it.
Next term:	*I am more than ever convinced . . . that the removal of that powerful personality, his brother, has left him free to develop his own, which is by no means cast in the same mould.*

Jon Snow (1947–)

Journalist, presenter of Channel 4 News

ST EDWARD'S, OXFORD, 1961–66

Warden's report, Winter 1962	*He does not give the impression of being an unintelligent boy. He has got plenty to say for himself, he is quite lively minded and he has got wide interest. The two things that are lacking, in my opinion, are the ability to concentrate and humility! He ought to be humble enough to recognise that he is the bottom boy in the slowest stream and that this is certainly not the right place for a boy of his ability . . .*
Form master, summer 1963	*He is not stupid but he has an errant concentration which lapses into apathy without much difficulty . . .* Maths: *He tries hard – but he can always be relied on to find whatever difficulties are going besides making a few up for himself.* French: *He has tried hard and, in spite of a tendency to muddle everything up, has made some good progress.* Art: *He tends to rely too much on mood and inspiration to stimulate his work. Pertinacity would show quicker dividends.*

History: *. . . He must learn to accept that his own ideas are not of equal value with those of the experts whose books he is instructed to read.*

Latin: *He gets into quite inexplicable muddles and is slow to desert a wrong conclusion . . . Unreliable: specious argument and attempts to defend his mistakes, rather than to correct them, take up time that would be better spent in accurate learning: time spent trying to eradicate these habits have seriously affected the progress of the rest of the form . . . one feels that he would never have been in the lowest of the fifths, had he learnt to learn humbly and not to question every point: he asks more than half the questions every period and about 90% of the unnecessary ones. It is time that he realized the selfishness of wasting everybody's time.*

. . . certainly there is no place for the aggressive question or a seemingly aggressive attitude.

Alan Rusbridger (1953–)

Editor, *The Guardian*

CRANLEIGH SCHOOL, 1967–72

Music	
	He has been very argumentative and contradictory this term. A certain degree of intellectual independence is quite healthy for a boy of his age, but when it comes to dismissing large numbers of facts as irrelevant and bringing in every type of specious argument to try and disprove them, I feel he has overstepped the mark. Had his written work been better, this would have had some justification, but his work has been generally of rather poor quality, and frequently missing altogether.
	Having said all this, I feel that if he can get a grip on himself, and adopt the attitude of one who wants to learn, rather than one who wants to argue, he still has the potential to do well.

Sue Lawley (1946–)

Presenter, Desert Island Discs

DUDLEY GIRLS' HIGH SCHOOL

PE	*I do believe Susan has glue in her plimsoles.*
English	*Susan would do well not to distract her friends during class. If she applied a quarter of the effort she puts into clowning, to her work, I venture to say she could be quite brilliant.*

Sue MacGregor CBE (1941–)

Presenter of Radio 4's *Today* programme for 18 years

HERSCHEL SCHOOL, CLAREMONT, CAPE PROVINCE,
SOUTH AFRICA

Upper Third, Head mistress's report	*Susan is not always good but she takes correction well.*
Sixth Form, Head mistress's report	*Her general manner is improving. She is less noisy and is always ready to help when asked. She must now endeavour to see the need for herself.*

Writers, Poets and Artists

'Vera should write some day'

on Vera Brittain, St Monica's,
Kingswood, Surrey, 1911

A. A. Milne (1882–1956)

Creator of Winnie the Pooh

WESTMINSTER SCHOOL, 1894

Aged 12	*Has done ill, showing little or no ambition, even in mathematics.*

Milne's reaction, and his father's, are recorded in Ann Thwaite's biography:

> When he read this Father turned his face to the wall, and abandoned hope. I, on the other hand, turned my face to the lighter side of life, and abandoned work . . . It was useless to point out to Father that the report was written before the result of the examinations, and that the examinations proved that the report was ridiculously wrong. Headmasters' reports couldn't be wrong. If Dr Rutherford said I had done ill, I had done ill.

Augustus John (1878–1961)
Painter
ST CATHERINE'S

Reports from John's first school, Greenhill, have not survived but the fact that they were very bad has. It seems that Augustus was a rebellious type and his behaviour was regularly reported to his father, who recorded them in a book. But he was forced to do more than commit 'Gussie's' misdeeds to paper when Augustus hit the second master. As biographer Michael Holroyd describes it:

> Having entered this last enormity in his ledger, he summoned Augustus to his study, read out the full catalogue of his crimes over the years and with a cry of 'Now, sir!' had, in his own words, 'recourse to the old-fashioned punishment of caning'.

He fared better at his next school, St Catherine's, whose headmaster described

the boldness and idealism of Augustus's aspirations.

P. G. Wodehouse (1881–1975)

Writer, creator of Jeeves and Wooster

DULWICH COLLEGE, 1899

General remarks	*He has done just fairly in the Summer examinations, but no more. I fear he has spent too much thought upon his cricket and the winning of colours.*
	He is a most impractical boy – continually he does badly in examinations from lack of the proper books; he is often forgetful; he finds difficulties in the most simple things and asks absurd questions, whereas he can understand the more difficult things.
	He has the most distorted ideas about wit and humour; he draws over his books and examination papers in the most distressing way and writes foolish rhymes in other people's books. Notwithstanding, he has a genuine interest in literature and can often talk with much enthusiasm and good sense about it. He does some things at times astonishingly well, and writes good Latin verses.
	He is a very useful boy in the school and in the VI form, and one is obliged to like him in spite of his vagaries. We wish him all success, and if he perseveres he will certainly succeed.

Rupert Brooke (1887–1915)

First World War Poet

RUGBY, 1900–1906

Winter term, 1900	*Conduct: Good. He has a standard of his own.*
Advent term, 1903	*Composition: promising (except for solecisms); some style and many blunders* *His foundations are most insecure . . . but he has taste and ability and I think he works. I hope he won't be content with being one of those boys who 'never can get up books'.* *More of a linguist than a thinker.*
Headmaster's report, Trinity term, 1906	*His work is more uneven than that of many boys in the form: he . . . dislikes details or has no facility for them. But where he is good . . . on the lively literary side of his work and in scholarship he is capable of very brilliant results . . . always a delightful boy to work with. I am very sorry to lose him.*

Seigfried Sassoon (1886–1967)

Poet

MARLBOROUGH, 1904

Headmaster's report	*Lacks power of concentration, shows no particular intelligence or aptitude for any branch of his work, seems unlikely to adopt any special career.*

Cyril Connolly (1903–1974)
Literary critic, journalist
ETON

Cyril Connolly was first at St Cyprian's with George Orwell (and Cecil Beaton). Both wrote about their school days, Orwell infamously in his 'Such, such were the joys' and Connolly in *Enemies of Promise*. Although Orwell's school reports have not survived it is thought to be his influence, at least according to Connolly's parents, which was responsible for the comment:

'cynical and irreverant'

in one of Connolly's Eton reports. They didn't get much better:

Maths: *His work like his hair is always unkempt, and, like his hands and face, frequently dirty. Indifference to personal appearance is no doubt a virtue but I cannot think it is good for a boy to be so grubby. It is certainly bad for his mathematics, in which he seems to have no ambition; otherwise a friendly and cheerful individual.*

Housemaster's report	*I have had sometimes to send him out of pupil room to wash his hands or change his very dirty collar – and I think he is old enough to have emerged from this grubby stage . . .*
	The boy certainly has a vein of great originality – he is very quick to see a point, thinks for himself with decided independence, criticises and comments well, and has a really remarkable gift for 'occasional' verse . . . But it is all very undisciplined at present.

He had obtained poor results

. . . in all work that calls for precise and accurate knowledge. And if his ability is to grow up to something better than cheap journalism he must tackle the training of it in habits of thoroughness and accuracy of thought.

He has a keen and a sincere mind but not one to which reverence comes very naturally. I do not think devotion comes easy to him . . . and he has not any romantic ideals – intellectually, for instance, his point of view is more that of a journalist than that of a scholar or scientist.

Cecil Beaton (1904–80)

Society photographer

HARROW

An indifferent academic career was summed up in this letter from the Head, Major Freeborn, to St John's College, Cambridge. Surprisingly, it got him a place.

As an artist he is quite exceptional and he is also good at English. During his time here, he won the Senior Reading Prize. With the ordinary school subjects such as Mathematics and Latin, he is very weak indeed, in fact, bad. He left Harrow at Easter to be coached for the 'Little Go' but I regret to say he has failed to get through. But he is a very nice boy and I feel sure you would not regret admitting him to the College for a degree. I believe he would read English and French perhaps, if one is able to take such a degree. During his last term, he was a House Monitor and was able to enforce his authority. At games he is quite useless and they do not appeal to him.

Graham Greene (1904–91)

Novelist

BERKHAMSTED SCHOOL, 1958
(where his father was Headmaster)

Housemaster, 1958	*The undoubted success he had on the stage [directing* Tons of Money*] in Memorial Hall shows that he is extremely capable at organizing other people, while the unsatisfactory reports in this folder show that he is not very capable at organizing himself. In the holidays he simply must get to grips with himself, and with his father's aid, must evolve a plan for his future.*

Greene writes about Berkhamsted School in *A Sort of Life*:

History was my favourite subject, and when I was about twelve a rather foolish master whom we all despised stated in my annual report, otherwise given up to laconic statements – 'satisfactory', 'tries hard', 'weak' and suchlike – that I 'had the makings of an historian'. I was pleased but considered rightly that it was an attempt to pander favour with my father.

Philip Larkin (1922–85)

Poet

KING HENRY VIII SCHOOL, COVENTRY, 1935–39

Larkin began well . . .

Headmaster's report	
1936	*Quite satisfactory. Would be better still if he would bring more enthusiasm to his work.*
1937	*Not very pleasing except in English. His literary subjects are very good, but he must work to strengthen weak subjects. Uneven and unlikely to pass School Certificate unless he devotes himself to the task of mastering certain uncongenial subjects.*
1938	*Tendency to foolishness must be checked.*

Dennis Potter (1935–94)

Playwright

ST CLEMENT DANES SCHOOL, LONDON

From the Head's report to Oxford where Potter gained a place at New College

> *He is extremely sensitive to the wrongs and injustices of the world as he sees them, but is able to conduct discussion and arguments with good humour and a growing tolerance of the opinions of others . . . Potter is a person of complete integrity of mind and character. He is a School Prefect and is meticulous in the performance of his duty . . .*

Richard Hoggart (1918–)

Scholar and writer of the influential *Uses of Literacy* (1957)

COCKBURN HIGH SCHOOL, LEEDS, 1930–36

Physics	*A capital all-round boy. Is developing along the right lines.*
English	*Very good: he works well, but there is a tendency to lose himself in words.*
1935	*. . . A most promising pupil. He is rapidly adapting himself to advanced work. His thoroughness is supported by powers of expression.*
Form master's report, 1936	*Very satisfactory. Has excellent ability and is a real plodder.*

Richard Hoggart sent this story with his reports:

The Headmaster had written at the bottom of the good report 'Should think of professional life'. My grandmother had no idea what that meant so she asked the Social Services visitor who brilliantly told her that it meant I could become a doctor or a clergyman. My grandmother was moved but worried. The visitor then went back to Social Services and persuaded them to increase my grandma's weekly payment for keeping me from 7/6 to 15/-; a moving turning point in my life!

Bruce Chatwin (1940–1989)

Travel writer and novelist

MARLBOROUGH, 1953

First term, 1953	Divinity: *He is somewhat dreamy and vague about the place and he might try to be less so – for our benefit.*
Lent, 1954	*Curiously patchy. His answers often contain considerable material, but the important point is missed.* Classics: *He must learn not to need to be the driver.* Biology: *I have failed to capture his interest.*
Roman history, Michaelmas, 1956	*. . . he finds difficulty in remembering facts and only the bizarre or trifling really appeals to him . . .* *He has a smooth and elegant style but is still too fond of the byways of historical accident. He would much sooner write an intimate memoir of Julius Caesar than a factual account of his Gallic wars. But then who would not? Unfortunately the examiners demand fact.*

Tom Paulin (1948–)

Poet

ANNADALE GRAMMAR SCHOOL

Lower Sixth Form, 1965

English Literature	*Excellent work in all papers. Perhaps a tendency to think of poetry philosophically rather than as literature. But once this is remedied he should do even better.*
History	*He takes an intelligent interest in the subject and shows a clear and deep understanding of events and movements. More factual detail would help.*

Margaret Forster (1938–)

Novelist, biographer

THE CARLISLE AND COUNTY HIGH SCHOOL FOR
GIRLS, 1956

English	*Margaret has worked with enthusiasm and determination. She has read widely, and can pronounce individual opinions upon the books.*
History	*Margaret has now so sure a grasp of her historical work that she can offer a critical judgement with assurance. Her interest is primarily in the interplay of personalities and she finds the more impersonal aspects of history less absorbing than one might expect from one of her ability.*
General report	*Margaret has enthusiasm and a capacity for hard and independent work. She must continue to apply herself to those aspects of her work which have neither dramatic nor stylistic qualities to capture her interest.*

Beryl Bainbridge (1934–)

Novelist, playwright

MERCHANT TAYLORS SCHOOL, CROSBY, c. 1943

English	*. . . though her written work is the product of an obviously lively imagination, it is a pity that her spelling derives from the same source.*
Geography	*Her knowledge of the subject is so poor as to make one wonder if she is simple-minded.*

Jilly Cooper (1938–)

Novelist

MOORFIELD SCHOOL, 1948, AND GODOLPHIN SCHOOL,
SALISBURY

Conduct	*Disappointing.*
General report	*Jill's work has been excellent this term – she has real ability and apart from her dreadful untidiness her progress has been entirely satisfactory.*
	She has a tremendous personality and must try hard not to let it make her intolerant. Individually her conduct has been delightful but in class most disappointing. I hope that next term she will try very hard to let her individual strength of character become a class delight to all.
at Godolphin	*Jilly has set herself an extremely low standard which she has failed to maintain.*

Helen Fielding (1958–)

Novelist, creator of Bridget Jones

WAKEFIELD GIRLS' HIGH SCHOOL (1962–1980)

Autumn 1963, age 5	*. . . Sometimes she simply observes and thinks. Her own conjectures can become so absorbing that she forgets time and the mundane necessities of classroom routine. Thus, her practical assistance is not necessarily valuable.*
Autumn 1964	*. . . Helen's free-writing is imaginative and some lively, often witty work is done. She has also recently progressed to combining neatness with interest.*
Senior School, English	*Helen must learn not to use such flowery language . . .*

Ken Follett (1949–)

Novelist

KITCHENER ROAD JUNIOR MIXED SCHOOL, CARDIFF,
1958 AND PRIESTMEAD PRIMARY JUNIOR MIXED
SCHOOL, KENTON, MIDDLESEX, 1960

Kitchener Road, July 1958	*Inclined to be troublesome and disobedient.*
and at Christmas 1958	*Inclined to be troublesome and disobedient.*
Then at Priestmead Primary	*Kenneth reads well, expresses himself well and accurately and is usually good at Arithmetic, but everything he does is spoiled by his attitude towards work and school, and by his bad behaviour. I hope he will be happy and successful in his new school but he must change his attitude to school life generally.*

Hunter Davies (1936–)

Journalist, writer, biographer

CARLISLE GRAMMAR SCHOOL, 1954

History	*Rather talkative.* *Untidy in mind as well as in handwriting at times. But he has worked well and keenly.*

Philip Pullman (1946–)

Novelist, winner of the Whitbread Prize 2002

YSGOL ARDUDWY, HARLECH, 1960

Look after the mind and the body will take care of itself. An almost perfect performance . . .

YSGOL ARDUDWY, HARLECH

REPORT for term ending 22nd December 1960

Name Pullman. Philip.   Form 3a

Number of Pupils in Form 33   Position in Form 3

Age 14 years 2 months   Average age of Form 13 years 10 months

No. of attendances made 141   No. of times absent 5   No. of times late

Subject	Terminal Examination			*Classwork			Remarks
	% of marks	Position	Average % of marks	Effort	Progress	Achievement	
Scripture	91	6	66	A	A	A	
History	62	11	24	A	A	A	
Geography	84	2/29	60	A	A	A	Very good Tom.
Welsh Language							
Welsh Literature							
English Language	85	1	60	A	A	A	Good. E.H.S
English Literature							
French 3 cd	87	2/24	62	A⁻	A	A	
Latin	88	1/23	63	A	A	A	
Mathematics Arithmetic	64	11	58	A	A	A	
Mathematics Algebra	85	3/25	60	A	A	A	
Mathematics Geometry	91	1/25	61	A	A	A	
Physics							
Chemistry							
Biology	68	13²	66	A	A	A	
Cookery				.			
Needlework or Woodwork							
Botany							
Zoology							
Art							
Music							
General Science							
Commerce or Metalwork							
Physical Education	C+			B	B	B	Can do better.

Conduct V. good   Neatness V. good

Remarks A very good report.

*A—Good ; B—Fair ; C—Weak.

Form Teacher I. J. Thomas

Headmaster W.E. Evans.

The next Term commences 10th January 1961

91

Howard Marks (1945–)

Writer and convicted drug smuggler

MC COUNTY INFANTS SCHOOL, 1953 AND GARW GRAMMAR SCHOOL, PONTYCYMER, GLAMORGAN, 1959

Aka Mr Nice, one of the hundreds of aliases used in the plying of Howard Marks' first trade: drug smuggling. Mr Nice was also the title of Marks' bestselling autobiography.

MC County Infants, general report	*Grade A – Excellent. A very good pupil in all his mental work and has improved in writing.*
Garw Grammar, form teacher's report	*Conduct very good. A very intelligent pupil who will do better when confidence and concentration increase.*

Robert Graves (1895–1985)

Poet, essayist, biographer, novelist

CHARTERHOUSE

Head's report on leaving, 1914	*Well, goodbye, Graves and remember that your best friend is the waste-paper basket.*

Statesmen and Women

'If ever I get into Parliament,' he muttered fiercely, 'I'll pass a lor against reports.'

William in *William and the School Report* by Richmal Crompton

One of the first letters that Alec Douglas-Home received upon taking up residence at No 10 Downing Street in October 1963 was from his Eton House Master, A. W. Whitworth, with whom he had maintained a warm friendship since his days there. Douglas-Home wrote back: 'You started it all!'

Although many showed their promise early on, it was not always so obvious that a future leader was under tuition.

Herbert H. Asquith (1852–1928)

Liberal Prime Minister 1908–1916

CITY OF LONDON SCHOOL, c. 1865

Aged 12, Headmaster's report	*There was nothing left but to place before him the opportunities of self-education and self-improvement, simply to put the ladder before him, and up he went.*

The Headmaster also commented on Asquith's oratory

. . . his speeches in the school debating society exhibited all the gravitas *and massive precision which were later to become recognised as the most notable Asquithian oratorical characteristics.*

Sir Winston Churchill (1874–1965)

Prime Minister 1940–45, 1951–55

ST GEORGE'S SCHOOL, ASCOT AND HARROW

St George's, first school report	*11th of 11 in form: He will do well but must treat his work in general more seriously next term . . . Very truthful, but a regular 'pickle' in many ways at present . . .*
Later report	*Is a constant trouble to everybody and is always in some scrape or other. He cannot be trusted to behave himself anywhere.*
Aged 9	*Very good abilities . . . He has no ambition – if he were really to exert himself he might yet be first at the end of term.*
Harrow	*Constantly late for school, losing his books and papers and various other things into which I need not enter. He is so regular in his irregularity that I really don't know what to do. He had such good abilities but these would be 'made useless by habitual negligence'.*

Churchill.

S. GEORGE'S SCHOOL,
ASCOT.

Report from _June 8th_ to _July 20th 1883_

Place in School Order	7th.	

<table>
<tr><td rowspan="5">Division Master's Classical Report.</td><td>Place in 4th Division of 9 Boys for ½ Term 9th.
Term 9th.</td><td></td></tr>
<tr><td>Composition</td><td>Very feeble.</td></tr>
<tr><td>Translation</td><td>Good.</td></tr>
<tr><td>Grammar</td><td>Improving. —</td></tr>
<tr><td>Diligence</td><td>Does not spirit understand the meaning of hard work — must make up his mind to do so next term</td></tr>
</table>

<table>
<tr><td rowspan="4">Set Master's Report.</td><td>Place in 3rd Set of 13 Boys for ½ Term 13th
Term 13th</td><td></td></tr>
<tr><td>Mathematics</td><td>Could do better than he does. —</td></tr>
<tr><td>French</td><td>fair</td></tr>
<tr><td>German</td><td>Total times late 19.</td></tr>
</table>

Scripture	⌠
History	very good.
Geography	very fair.
Writing and Spelling	Writing good but so terribly slow. — Spelling about as bad as it well can be.
Music	—
Drawing	— _H. Martin Cooke._
General Conduct	improved. —

Herbert Kynnersley Head Master.

St George's, aged 7

99

So critical were Winston's reports that Lady Randolph was forced to react. On receipt of a particularly bad report from the Headmaster, Churchill's mother wrote to her son: sentiments many a parent today might well share.

Dear Winnie

I have much to say to you, I'm afraid not of a pleasant nature. You know darling how I hate to find fault with you, but I can't help myself this time . . .

You work in such a fitful way that you are bound to come last – look at your place in the form! Your father & I are both more disappointed than one can say, that you are unable to go up for preliminary exam: I daresay you have a 1000 excuses for not doing so – but there the fact remains! If only you had a better place in your form & were a little more methodical I should try and find an excuse for you.

Dearest Winston you make us very unhappy – I had built up such hopes around you & felt so proud of you & now all is gone – my only consolation is that your conduct is good, & that you are an affectionate son – but your work is an insult to your intelligence – If you would trace out a plan of action for yourself & carry it out & be determined to do so – I am sure you could accomplish anything. It is that thoughtlessness of yours which is your greatest enemy & your Father threatens to send you with a tutor off somewhere for the holidays. I can assure you it will take a great deal to pacify him & I do not know how it is to be done – I must say I think you repay his kindness to you very badly. There is Jack on the other hand who comes at the head of class every . . .

I will say no more now but Winston you are old enough to see how serious this is to you & how the next year or two & the use you make of them, will affect your whole life – Stop and think it out for yourself & take a good pull before it is too late . . .

Your loving but distressed Mother

Her heartfelt pleas seemed to have done the trick.

Age 18, on leaving	*His work this term has been excellent. He understands now the need of taking trouble, and the way to take it and, whatever happens to him [possibly a reference to him sitting for the second time (and failing again) exams for Sandhurst] I shall consider that in the last twelve months he has learned a lesson of life-long value.*

Churchill, in 1930

I am all for the Public schools, but I do not want to go there again.

Clement Attlee (1883–1967)

First British Labour Prime Minister to form a majority government 1945–51

HAILEYBURY, 1896

Housemaster's report	*He thinks about things and forms opinions – a very good thing . . . I believe him a sound character and think he will do well in life. His chief fault is that he is very self-opinionated, so much so that he gives very scant consideration to the views of other people.*

On the bottom of the Haileybury report were five divisions – Good, Moderate, No Complaint, Indifferent and Bad, with a space in each division for the Headmaster to sign. For the whole time he was at Haileybury Atlee scored only 'No Complaint', except for the last term's report, in 1901, when he rose to a 'Moderate'.

Sir Alec Douglas-Home (1903–1995)

Conservative Prime Minister 1963–64

LUDGROVE, WOKINGHAM AND ETON, 1917–22

On leaving Ludgrove in 1917 for Eton	*I am delighted about Alec and he deserves great credit for having worked with such keenness and perseverance. I shall miss him very much, but I hope he will be very happy and get on well at Eton in every way, which I am sure he will. Alec has won the racquet cup and fives cup, so is ending his career here in a blaze of glory.*
Eton, July 1922	*I have never heard him grumble or criticize harshly anybody or anything since he came here and so he has been head of what I think has all the year been a very happy family . . . He has sound ability quite enough to enable him with his other gifts to attain real success and power even in public life. But he is not at present ambitious and not inclined to go out and face storms from which he can stand aside.*

Sir Alec Douglas-Home is the only Prime Minister ever to have played First Class Cricket, appearing occasionally for Middlesex, 1924–5.

Sir Stafford Cripps (1889–1952)

Clement Attlee's Chancellor 1947

WINCHESTER COLLEGE

Housemaster's report	*Loveable and disarms hostility; liked and respected by all the boys.*
Headmaster's report	*I have an encouraging report about your boy's work . . . he seems to me to be shaping up into a really strong candidate for a scholarship. The point is that the boy is developing well and has an intelligent interest in his subject . . . He has been doing some English reading and writing for me, chiefly on Bagehot's Physics and Politics. I find he is quite good in getting the main point of what he reads, but needs a good deal more practice in setting out his point, leading up to it and seeing what follows from it. I shall give him a great deal more practice in this presently. He is a thoroughly good fellow.*

Cripps turned down the offered place at New College, Oxford in favour of the scholarship place he'd won at University College London studying chemistry. This is the report from Science don W. B. Croft to Cripps'

father:

[he] has been working in the right way; his eyes fixed not always on the prize but usually a little beyond that, entering into the love and enthusiasm for the subject which belongs to it. Without this feeling school exercises are often an injury to the mind . . . The examiners spoke with enthusiasm about your son's work. I should like also to commend his habits of readiness and punctuality which quietly add to the power of good abilities.

To which the Headmaster added:

I can only say that I told the Warden of New College he is a fellow of quite first rate ability. But better than all that, he is a fellow of real high purpose and genuine appreciation – I respect and like him very much.

Sir Anthony Eden (1897–1977)

Conservative Prime Minister 1955–57

SANDROYD, c. 1910 AND ETON, 1912

Headmaster's report	*He is rather young for his years still and wants more determination to go his own way. He has begun to develop in this way. His soft heart balanced by a little more grit and energy will make a strong as well as a lovable character of him.*
At Eton, July 1912, from his House Tutor, E. L. Churchill	*So at present he is at any rate a son of whom you may be quite proud. Of course he will not get through life without giving us some anxiety. But for the moment I veritably think there is no cause for any at all and a great deal of cause for satisfaction with him.*

However, through the course of 1913, Eden seems to have caused Churchill anxiety over his 'inattention, untidiness, and forgetfulness' and 'his tantrums' and 'fits of inattention and slackness'. But, this passed:

July 1913	*He has quite ceased to be petulant or childish, and is getting much more thoughtful and steady. As I have said before, he is a very good boy, and I like him. His weakness was – I am not at all sure that it is fair to say is – a certain heedlessness and lack of restraint. That seems to be becoming a thing of the past, and I hope you no longer find him in any way difficult to manage in the holidays, and that he has grown out of the 'tantrums' of which he used to give exhibitions from time to time at home.*

Eden never really liked Eton or, at least, was indifferent to it and was eager to leave and join the war effort. Churchill was aghast:

> You fool, you won't be any use at the war, but you could be of some help in the House four.

Lady Margaret Thatcher (1925–)
Conservative Prime Minister 1979–1990
KESTEVEN AND GRANTHAM GIRLS' SCHOOL, 1936

Form report	*Margaret has worked steadily and well throughout the term. She has definite ability, and her cheeriness makes her a very pleasant member of her form. Her behaviour is excellent.*
Fourth year	*. . . more than usual depth of understanding . . . showing the makings of a real student. She thinks clearly and logically, and expresses herself well in writing.*
Final report	*Margaret is ambitious and deserves to do well.*

John Maynard Keynes (1883–1946)

Economist and member of the Bloomsbury Group

ETON, 1897–1902

The mathematical ability of the man who went on to devise his influential economic theory was spotted very early:

Perse Girls' School, Cambridge.

KINDERGARTEN TRANSITION CLASS.

Name *Maynard Keynes*   Report for term ending *Dec. 19th* 1890

Holy Scripture	*Shews keen interest*
Reading	*Improving, but needs care*
Writing	*Has made progress.*
Arithmetic	*Very much improved, shews power.*
History	*Very good indeed.*
Geography	
Nature Lesson	*Good*
Drawing	*Fair*
K. G. Occupations	*Geometrical Paper-Folding Shews intelligent interest*
General Remarks	*Is working very well.*
Conduct	*Very good.*

December 1897	*. . . Still with him as with all able boys there is the danger that the extreme ease with which he fulfils all that is required of him, may lead him to be satisfied with the ordinary standards of his everyday work. There is no doubt of his energy and ambition: but I would like in certain things, to see him a little more dissatisfied, a little more ready to note the points in which he fails.*
Eton, Classical report, Lent, 1898	*Has done admirable work in almost everything, construing excellent questions, very thoughtful, good and well-expressed. History began middling and steadily improved. I hope that the more accurate sciences will not dry the readiness of his sympathy and insight for more inspiring and human subjects: his title essay on 'Antigone' was not like the work of one made for Mathematics. He has a well-furnished and delightful mind.*

April, 1900	*. . . no amount of floods, illness, bad weather has in the least degree interfered with the steady rigorous course of his work.*
On leaving for King's Cambridge in 1902	*He leaves regretted by everyone who knows him. He has I think been lucky in his time here: the leading boys here during the last year or two seem to me to have been extremely nice: and well has he taken his part among them. He has no doubt a very fine mature mind, and he is not in the least overweighted by it as many boys of his age might be; I have rarely known any boy so clever, and yet so far removed from any trace of priggishness . . . I fear it may be long before I have again a pupil who will combine ability and industry so well; of his character I will only say that I think he is a boy on whom one can depend entirely. With all his cleverness he accepts the duties put before him with the readiest obedience and without any questioning as to whether he himself after all does not know best.*

Lord Longford (1905–2001)

Labour politician and social reformer

ETON, c. 1922

Longford was at Eton at the same time as Alec Douglas-Home. He had a much less glittering career there.

At first	*a very clever boy who can talk Latin with some fluency*
but then	*His whole life consists in a more or less elaborate pretence. His written work is indescribably filthy. Considering his obvious abilities his place is discreditable.*
Final report	*He is no longer such a contented dweller in Philistia*

Franklin D. Roosevelt (1882–1945)
Thirty-second President of the USA 1932–45
GROTON SCHOOL, MASSACHUSETS, 1896–1900

Headmaster's report, Reverend Endicott Peabody, final year	*He has been a thoroughly faithful scholar and a most satisfactory member of this school throughout his course. I part with Franklin with reluctance.*

The Rev Peabody stayed close to Roosevelt throughout the rest of his life, officiating at his marriage to Eleanor and participating in Roosevelt's inaugural church services in Washington.

Eleanor Roosevelt (1884–1962)

American First Lady, wife of Franklin D. Roosevelt

ALLENSWOOD, LONDON, 1899

Allenswood was an international school which had relocated from Paris to Wimbledon.

At the end of her first year, 1899	*Excellent. She is the most amiable girl I have ever met; she is nice to everybody, very eager to learn and highly interested in all her work.*
Then in a letter to Eleanor's grandmother (her guardian)	*All that you said when she came here of the purity of her heart, the nobleness of her thought has been verified by her conduct among people who were at first perfect strangers to her . . . I often found that she influenced others in the right direction. She is full of sympathy for all those who live with her and shows an intelligent interest in everything she comes in contact with.*
	As a pupil she is very satisfactory, but even that is of small account when you compare it with the perfect quality of her soul.

Dwight D. Eisenhower (1890–1969)

General and thirty-fourth President of the USA 1952–60

US MILITARY ACADEMY, 1915

Efficiency Report from Lieutenant Colonel Morton F. Smith, Commandant of Cadets	*Attention to duty, habits, general bearing, military appearance, and attitude toward discipline, very good. Cadet rank: 3rd Class, Corporal; 2nd Class Private; 1st Class, Colour Sergeant. Activity and athletic standing (gymnasium, football and other sports) athletic. Horsemanship, excellent. Marksmanship, Sharpshooter. Swordsmanship, fair. Choice of Arm of Service, Infantry, Coast Artillery, Cavalry. General abilities for an officer in the army, judgement, originality, energy, efficiency and character very good; should be assigned to organization under strict commanding officer.*

John F. Kennedy (1917–63)

Thirty-fifth President of the USA 1960–63
THE CHOATE SCHOOL, MASSACHUSETS, c. 1932

For the Fourth Quarter	*I'd like to take responsibility for Jack's constant lack of natness (sic) about his room and person, since he lived with me for two years. But in the matter of neatness, despite a genuine effort on Jack's part, I must confess to failure.*
	Occasionally we did manage to effect a house cleaning, but it necessitated my 'dumping' everything in the room into a pile in the middle of the floor. Jack's room has throughout the year been subject to instant and unannounced inspection – it was the only way to maintain a semblance of neatness, for Jack's room was a club for his friends.
	I regard the matter of neatness or lack of it on Jack's part as quite symbolic – aside from the value it has in itself – for he is casual and disorderly in almost all of his organization projects. Jack studies at the last minute, keeps appointments late, has little sense of material value, and can seldom locate his possessions.
	Despite all this, Jack has had a thoroughly genuine try at being neat according to his own standards and he has been almost religiously on time through the Quarter.
	I believe Jack began to sense the fitness of things after his midwinter difficulties, and he has and is trying to be a more socially minded person.

Jimmy Carter (1924–)

Thirty-ninth President of the USA (1976–80)

PLAINS HIGH, GEORGIA, 1935

REPORT OF													
Carter, Jimmy													
MONTHS	1	2	3	4	Ex	Av	5	6	7	8	9	Ex	Av	Y.av
DAYS PRESENT	20	20	20	20		80	20	20	20	20		80	160
TIMES TARDY	1	0	0	0		1		1	1			2	3
CONDUCT	a	a	a	a		a	a	a	a	a		a	a
SPELLING	a	a	a	a		a	a	a	a	a		a	a
READING	a	a	a	a		a	u	a	a	a		a	a
WRITING	a	a	a	a		a	a	a	a	a		a	a
ARITHMETIC	a	a	a	a		a	a	a	a	a		a	a
GRAMMAR	a	a	a	a		a	a	a	a	a		a	a
LANGUAGE													
GEOGRAPHY	a	a	a	a		a	a						a
HISTORY							a	a	a	a		a	a
HEALTH	a	a	a	a		a	a	a	a	a		a	a
DRAWING													
MUSIC	a	a	a	a		a	43	a	c		B	a
AGRICULTURE													
Teeth	o.k.	o.k.	o.k.				o.k.	o.k.	o.k.	o.k.		o.k.	O.K.

Straight 'A's and teeth 'ok' . . .

117

George Bush (1924–)

Forty-first President of the USA (1988–92)

US ARMY REPORT, 1943

Fitness Report for Student Officers and Cadets				
Outstanding	*3.9 to 3.8*	*Below average*	*3.1 to 2.5*
Above average	*3.7 to 3.5*	*Unsatisfactory*	*2.4 to 2.0*
Average	*3.4 to 3.2*	*Inferior*	*1.9 to 1.0*

Name: Bush, G. H.

Intelligence	*3.3*	*Loyalty*	*3.0*
Judgment	*3.2*	*Perserverance*	*3.3*
Initiative	*3.3*	*Reactions in emergencies*	*3.3*
Force	*3.2*	*Endurance*	*3.3*
Moral Courage	*3.2*	*Military bearing, neatness*	
Cooperation	*3.0*	*of dress and person*	*3.6*
		Industry	*3.6*

Instructor's comments:

Aviation Cadet Bush is an upstanding lad with great self-confidence. It appears, however, that he may be somewhat eccentric.

Air Marshal Ian Macfadyen (1942–)

RAF Fighter Pilot & Lieutenant Governor, Isle of Man

ST PIRAN'S, MAIDENHEAD

Headmaster's report **Winter term, 1956** **Housemaster's report, 1959**	*. . . Shot very well this term, and was just runner-up for the shooting cup.* *He was top of the set at half-term: after that his deterioration was catastrophic.* *He's reliable, cheerful and energetic as ever. It is good to have in House someone who is so determined to make the best of things, who doesn't grumble, and who consequently gets the maximum value from everything.*

Arthur M. Schlesinger, Jr. (1917–)

Historian and political appointee to J. F. Kennedy

EXETER SCHOOL, MASSACHUSETS, c. 1930

Principal's report to Harvard admissions office	*A tall, slender, stalk of a boy with a face illuminated by intelligence and adolescent joys. Earnest and devoted to his studies, with genuine intellectual interest going beyond the limits of the class-room. He is really concerned about the affairs of the world outside the school. He has an attractive personality and many friends.*

Arthur Schlesinger's reaction (as quoted in his autobiography):

I was not, alas, very tall and can only hope that the rest of the report was more reliable.

Viscount Montgomery of Alamein

('Monty') (1887–1976)

British Field Marshal

ST PAUL'S, LONDON, c. 1902

Form Master's report, aged 18	*. . . sometimes strange . . . backward . . . no notion of style. . . . rather backward for his age. To have a serious chance for Sandhurst, he must give more time to work.*
Then, his final report in 1906	*Chemistry: slow to grasp principles* *Mathematics: his knowledge is weak* *French: still backward*

The comment 'still somewhat backward' was deleted by the High Master of St Paul's on the version sent to his parents.

Lord Louis Mountbatten (1900–1979)
Last Viceroy of India, 1947

MR GLADSTONE'S, CLIVEDEN PLACE, c. 1909 AND LOCKER'S PARK SCHOOL, BERKHAMSTED

Mr Gladstone's, first term	*Spelling weak, at times weird. Conduct excellent. Works well and is getting on.*

He started off at Locker's Park School 'in a very half-hearted way' but gradually settled in:

> *He has maintained his high standard of industry . . . his keen enthusiasm in work and games, his sense of humour and his modesty make him increasingly popular with boys and masters.*

Lord Michael Heseltine (1933–)
Conservative MP and Cabinet Minister in Margaret Thatcher's government
SHREWSBURY

In his biography of Heseltine, Michael Crick reports on a rather vicious Old Salopian tradition. The monitor of each house study, that is a senior boy, wrote what were known as 'faste', or internal reports on the younger boys.

> *He is rebellious, objectionable, idle, imbecilic, inefficient, antagonizing, untidy, lunatic, albino, conceited, inflated, impertinent, underhand, lazy and smug.*

To which was added:

> *cheerful and probably rudimentally good-natured.*

Fortunately, his teachers were slightly less brutal.

Final report	*An interesting boy. I hope that his academic success, which has not been inconsiderable, will have led him to realize what a lot most of us do not know. He has considerable potentialities still, I feel.*

Michael Foot (1913–)

Historian, politician and Leader of the Labour Party 1980–83

PLYMOUTH COLLEGE AND FORRES SCHOOL, SWANAGE

Got excellent school reports in all subjects, including History:

> *He remembers every detail of the stories.*

Then, at Forres, a letter from the Headmaster to his father on leaving:

> *We shall miss Michael sadly. He has been the leading boy in the school in every way . . . and we have no hesitation at all in saying he must have the highest honour we can pay him, by putting his name on the Honours Board . . . What he does will not lack a spirit of grit and keenness behind it – and I think he will always have the right ideals in view.*

He was also:

> *Rugger: a good wing forward*
> *Cricket: a promising batsman*

Lord Ashdown (1941–)

(Jeremy John Dunham 'Paddy' Ashdown)

Former Leader of the Liberal Democrats

BEDFORD SCHOOL, 1952–59

Headmaster's report	*Except that he was a trifle impulsive and often wanted to reorganize something at a moment's notice, he made an excellent Head of House. Infectious enthusiasm and good spirited, he carried the whole House with him and it ran smoothly and very happily. He could express his own view-point well and fearlessly but would always accept another point of view when he had heard the arguments in its favour. An excellent leader, quite unbigoted, and patient, so that he was popular with everyone but at the same time set an example in nearly everything he did.*
Games	*A good fellow, if a bit excessively Irish at times . . .*

John Redwood (1951–)

Conservative MP

KENT COLLEGE, CANTERBURY, 1968

Divinity	*Once and for all I must say what a pleasure it has been to know him and to share a little in his studies and his thinking. I admire his high standards of both scholarship and behaviour. I hope that experience will show him new excellencies and perfections – and deepen that great kindness which he already has at heart. I wish him every happiness.*
Economics	*His work has been outstanding. He has studied some aspects of the subject in great depth with very impressive results. It has been a great pleasure to share in his studies, and I wish him well. I hope we shall not entirely lose contact.*
English	*While he was able to approach the examination with a certain gay abandon, he worked steadily and conscientiously at the texts and, I believe, has reaped his own reward in his heightened appreciation and enjoyment resulting from detailed knowledge.* *I should like to express my personal gratitude for all he has contributed.*

History	*I very much enjoyed reading his project and have been very impressed by and grateful for his contribution in form. The history section of the library will miss his supervision. I wish him all the best for the future.*
Headmaster's final report	*He has come to the end of a most successful school career and we can express only gratitude to him for all he has contributed to the School and for the fine examples he has set by his industry and scholarship. We are confident that he has a bright academic future and we shall follow his career with interest.*
	Excellent work in every way. He has pursued his own studies with his usual thoroughness and continued to set an admirable example in scholarship and critical acumen. I have thoroughly enjoyed working with him.

Lord David Owen (1938–)

Former Joint Leader of the Liberal Democrats

MOUNT HOUSE & BRADFIELD COLLEGE

Mount House Head's report, final year	*If I had to select an expedition to go to the South Pole he would be the first person I would choose. But I would make sure that he was not on the return journey!*
Bradfield College	*Can be a scruffy urchin, must be a decent citizen. Rare moral courage has not made him a prig.*

Lord David Steel (1938–)

Former Joint Leader of the LibDems and Leader of the Scottish Parliament

PRINCE OF WALES SCHOOL, NAIROBI, KENYA, 1950–53

PE	*He plays a fair game of hockey for the Remainders.*

Inventors, Explorers, Innovators and Other Movers and Shakers

A curious catch-all category where scientists and spies rub shoulders with princesses and sportsmen. The common denominator is that somehow or other these people have all made an impact.

I would have liked to have had a single category of some of these, especially, for example, sportsmen and women. But apart from a charming refusal from Lennox Lewis and an almost daily email report on Ellen MacArthur's progress round whatever ocean she's conquering now, I failed to unearth much on the early academic years of our sporting heroes.

John Polanyi (1929–)

Nobel Prize winner, Chemistry 1986

MANCHESTER GRAMMAR SCHOOL, 1946

Form master's report	*Though he seems to view his schoolmasters with amused and olympian contempt, the present illusion of a superior mind is usually shattered by a display of abominable ignorance. He is a lazy observer and lazy in acquiring the solid factual foundations of knowledge. He could work hard.*

Paul Nurse (1949–)

Director of the Imperial Cancer Research Fund and winner of the Nobel Prize in 2001

HARROW COUNTY SCHOOL FOR BOYS, 1960–66

In contrast to his fellow Laureate John Polanyi, Paul Nurse received generally outstanding reports culminating with this on his Sixth Form report.

Form master	*I hope he will be satisfied with nothing less than the very best.*
Headmaster	*He must continue to aim high.*

He did.

Sir Ranulph Fiennes OBE (1944–)

Explorer

SANDROYD AND ETON, 1957

Ranulph Fiennes went up to Eton in 1957 with the following report:

Ranulph Fiennes goes on to Eton where it is suggested he will soon be leading a gang! Be that as it may he will certainly make his mark as he has made it here. The combination of his histrionic ability, imagination, humour and leadership could hardly fail to attract attention. No doubt his talent for telling ghost (and other) stories will also come in useful.

And with this report on his football career:

Characters of the 1st XI	*Spoiled much of his real usefulness by hanging back but showed real ability from time to time.*

Dame Stella Rimington (1935–)

Former (and first female) head of MI5

NOTTINGHAM HIGH SCHOOL FOR GIRLS, 1947–54

The following comments were made by teachers on Stella's record card:

> *Stella is very ready to contribute her share in school affairs.*
>
> *Stella is a most helpful member of her form.*
>
> *With a more consistent effort, Stella could do well.*
>
> *Stella has ability. She must determine to make fullest possible use of it.*

In addition, her record shows that she was games captain for her form, played in the second hockey XI and edited her form magazine, and her interests are listed as swimming, rowing, classical music, dancing, hiking and reading. In the Sixth Form she was elected a School Prefect, Form Representative, Joint Secretary to the School Dramatic Society and she stage managed the school play, *St Joan*, 'most competently'. Last but not least, she was property cupboard prefect!

J. Edgar Hoover (1895–1972)

Head of the FBI for nearly fifty years

BRENT ELEMENTARY SCHOOL, WASHINGTON DC, 1901

J. Edgar was a star student at Brent, where he began his school career in 1901, receiving excellent reports in all subjects. Perhaps more note-worthy is his own habit of writing reports on the teachers in his leather-bound notebook:

> Miss Hinckle, 4th Grade, who raised me in discipline . . . Miss Snowden who raised me intellectley [sic] . . . Miss Dalton, 8th Grade, a fine lady who raised me morally . . .

Diana, Princess of Wales (1961–1997)

RIDDLESWORTH AND WEST HEATH SCHOOLS

From Riddlesworth	*Diana has been outstandingly helpful this term. She has proved herself efficient and a good organizer. If only she would put the same enthusiasm into her work, she could move mountains. There are occasional lapses when she becomes rather quarrelsome but these are much fewer than in the past.*
From West Heath	*She must try to be less emotional in her dealings with others.*

Duchess of Windsor (1896–1986)

formerly Wallis Simpson

OLDFIELDS

The Duchess of Windsor went to what was really a finishing school, a boarding school called Oldfields; its motto was 'Gentleness and courtesy at all times'.

In keeping with the spirit of this motto, there were two rival basketball teams, one named Gentleness and one Courtesy. The Duchess of Windsor played guard for Gentleness. But although she took part in the games, she drew the line at Algebra and went to some lengths to avoid it. She wrote to her mother saying she would die if she had to take it, and she was excused. Her mother wrote:

> extreme nervousness induced by prolonged exposure to mathematics gave Wallis the hives

Reports home were, nonetheless, favourable:

31 March 1914	*My dear Mrs Rasin*
	We will give Wallis the privilege of going into town on Wednesday afternoon on the 2.20 train to have her skirt fitted.
	She has been such a faithful student and her averages have been so good we feel that she deserves some extra privilege.

Carl Gustav Jung (1875–1961)
Psychoanalyst

was

all glib cleverness and humbug

according to his German teacher in reaction to an essay that Jung had troubled over, as he didn't usually.

Isaiah Berlin (1909–97)

Political scientist, philosopher

ST PAUL'S SCHOOL, LONDON, c. 1922

He is sometimes inclined to write about ultimates, instead of addressing himself to the question in hand.

One teacher, remarking on Berlin's schoolboy review of a London performance of *The Cherry Orchard*, detected the

hint of superiority which even if you possess . . . you should hide.

A. J. Ayer (1910–89)

Philosopher

ETON, 1923

Form master's report	*A bumptious, aggressive, difficult boy, too pleased with his own cleverness.*

and

Ayer's problem was that he never knew when he was not wanted.

John Arlott (1914–1991)

Cricket writer and broadcaster

QUEEN MARY'S GRAMMAR SCHOOL

The stinging remarks of an English teacher, as reported in a biography of his father by his son, Tim:

> W. H. 'Boney' Pearce, holding aloft one of a classmate and friend of Arlott, Jack Donovan's, essays and one of my father's, said: 'Donovan, you will make a living with your pen. Arlott, I don't know why you bother.'

Richard Dunwoody MBE (1964–)

Champion jockey

RENDCOMB COLLEGE, NEAR CHELTENHAM, 1979

History	*Accurate and intelligent work, and he keeps a splendid notebook.*
House tutor's report	*An excellent report. Well done indeed! I must say, more out of a sense of duty than concern, that Richard's O level effort must not be allowed to relax. I see a crop of A grades on the horizon – there for the taking.*

In Fiction

With a sigh of relief Mr Carter noticed that there was only one more end-of-term report to be done: J. C. T. Jennings. But Mr Carter wasn't quite sure what to say about Jennings. When Mr Carter cast his mind back over the more hair-raising events of Jennings' first term, it seemed that Jennings was behind most of them . . .

From *Jennings Goes to School* by Anthony Buckeridge

It isn't surprising that the report, with its ominous air of inevitability and retribution (not to mention injustice) should have become a tool for the writers of public – and other – school fiction. In a very early incarnation, the report had a role in advancing the story in Thomas Hughes's *Tom Brown's Schooldays*:

Then the last Saturday, on which the Doctor came round to each form to give out the prizes, and hear the masters' last report of how they and their charges had been conducting themselves; and Tom, to his huge delight, was praised, and got his remove into the lower fourth, in which all his School-house friends were.

143

The report can come in handy as a straightforward twist to end a plot, such as in *Billy Bunter of Greyfriars School* by Frank Richards. The Fat Owl of the Remove has gorged and lied and misbehaved his merry way through the preceding chapters, prompting the threat of expulsion. But finally, after a jape involving a sack of soot, Bunter fortuitously falls out of a tree and onto a mugger who is about to attack his form master, Mr Quelch:

> 'You have been very courageous, Bunter.'
>
> 'Oh!'
>
> 'And I want you to know just how grateful I am.'
>
> 'Oh!' gasped Bunter again, hardly able to take it in. Was Quelch actually praising him?
>
> 'I shall certainly mention it in my end of term report . . . and I shall not advise your father to remove you from Greyfriars.'

Richmal Crompton's William Brown goes one better than those real-life scallywags Neil Kinnock and Auberon Waugh, by not only destroying his school report before his parents see it but, inventive as ever, turning it to his own advantage. His father is forced to accord him leniency when he learns of how William has impressed his old, rich Aunt Augusta by sacrificing his (very bad) school report to a paper trail in a bogus rescue attempt. Together they try to recover the pieces and put them back together again:

Aunt Augusta picked up the 'oo' of 'poor' and said, 'This must be a 'good', of course.' She picked up the 'ex' of 'extremely lazy and inattentive' and said, 'This must be an 'excellent', of course.' But even Aunt Augusta realized that it would be impossible to put together all the pieces.

'I'm afraid it can't be done, dear,' she said sadly. 'How disappointing for you. I know just what you are feeling, dear boy.'

William, hoping that she didn't, hastily composed his features to their expression of complacent modesty tinged with deep disappointment – the expression of a boy who has had the misfortune to lose a magnificent school report . . .

In *The Mile* by George Layton, the main character's chagrin at a terrible school report is mitigated by the knowledge that the time he could have spent at lessons has been ploughed into a successful bid to best a bully. It's only that secret knowledge that gets him through this inquisition, when his mother reads the end-of-term verdict.

My mum was reading the report for the third time. She put it down on the table and stared at me. I didn't say anything. I just stared at my gammon and chops and pineapple ring. What could I say? My mum looked so disappointed. I really felt sorry for her. She was determined for me to do well at school, and get my 'O' Levels, then get my 'A' Levels, then go to university, then get my degree, and then get a good job with good prospects . . .

'I'm sorry, Mum . . .'

She picked up the report again, and started reading it for the fourth time.

'It's no good reading it again, Mum. It's not going to get any better.'

She slammed the report back on to the table.

145

'Don't you make cheeky remarks to me. I'm not in the mood for it!'

I hadn't meant it to be cheeky, but I suppose it came out like that.

'I wouldn't say anything if I was you, after reading this report!'

I shrugged my shoulders.

'There's nothing much I can say, is there?'

'You can tell me what went wrong. You told me you worked hard this term!'

I had told her I'd worked hard, but I hadn't.

'I did work hard, Mum.'

'Not according to this.'

She waved the report under my nose.

'You're supposed to be taking your 'O' Levels next year. What do you think is going to happen then?'

I shrugged my shoulders again, and stared at my gammon and chips.

'I don't know.'

She put the report back on the table. I knew I hadn't done well in my exams because of everything that had happened this term, but I didn't think for one moment I'd come bottom in nearly everything. Even Norbert Lightowler had done better than me.

'You've come bottom in nearly everything. Listen to this.'

She picked up the report again.

'"Maths – Inattentive and lazy."'

I knew what it said.

'I know what it says, Mum.'

She leaned across the table and put her face close to mine.

' I know what it says too, and I don't like it.'

She didn't have to keep reading it.

'Well, stop reading it then.'

My mum just gave me a look.

'"English Language – He is capricious and dilettante." What does that mean?'

I turned the pineapple ring over with my fork. Oh heck, was she going to go through every rotten subject?

'Come on – English Language – Mr Melrose says you're "capricious and dilettante". What does he mean?'

'I don't know!'

I hate Melrose. He's really sarcastic. He loves making a fool of you in front of other people. Well, he could stick his 'capricious and dilettante', and his rotten English Language, and his set books and his horrible breath that nearly knocks you out when he stands over you.

'I don't know what he means.'

'Well, you should know. That's why you study English Language, to understand words like that. It means you mess about, and don't frame yourself.'

My mum kept reading every part of the report over and over again. It was all so pointless. It wasn't as if reading it over and over again was going to change anything.

. . . She put the report back into the envelope. Hurray! The Spanish Inquisition was over. She took it out again. Trust me to speak too soon.

'I mean, you didn't even do well at sport, did you? "Sport – He is not a natural athlete." Didn't you do anything right this term?'

Apart from destroying it, or suffering the consequences, there's the cruder option of the DIY report, as suggested in *How to be Topp* by Geoffrey Willans:

147

The Molesworth Bogus Report

ST. CUSTARDS.

NAME n. molesworth

EXAM ORDER   ❚   TERM ORDER   ❚

FINAL ORDER   ❚

SUBJECT	POSITION	REMARKS
History	I	Extraordinary! His life of Marlborough was uncannily brilliant one of the best things of its kind in the present century. GUB
Geog.	1	We have a splendid sense of position. Give him a globe and he know exactly what do with it. P. rt. I. gs
Latin	1	It is seldom that we get a skolar like this who knows all his grammer backwards. If he have a fault it is too much quickness diry eares. I wish did not write enuff for him but would be better if he thought things write in latin B.E.9.K
Greek	1	Beyond words B. EAK
English	1 (ONE)	I didn't ought too say to much in praise of his style did I but his essays are remarkable and have been reproduced in skool mag. coe strikes a flipin like a genius S.T.E
French	1 (UNE)	Tres, tres tres tres tres très bien. Bravo! Formidable. M.U.D.

Directions: Fill in the name and post on first day of hols.
Destroy reel report when it comes along.

SUBJECT	POSITION	REMARKS
Drawing	1	A wonderful sense of colour + line. His choice of subjects is perhaps a little doubtful. F.V.C
Music	1#	Tarcanarini must beware. Benjamin Britten

HEADMASTERS REPORT

There was a time when dere nigel was rather wild and chased about the place at full tilt shouting "Down with skool!". Now thanks to St Custard's that is all changed Turanks to St custard's he have almost worked a miracle—now we see him whole sledar, poet, man of action—dilletaste, wine lover, dreamer, beer drinker—coiner of frazes, wit, athlete, strongman. He is the LOT. (thanks to St Custard's) I think he should now goon from strength to strength and you can imagine with what feelings I look forward to his returning next term.

J. Duddridge Plunk

| Next term begins* : | Jan. .... May .... Sept. **31**. | (Headmaster & sole Licensee) |

MATRON'S REPORT

We forgot to pack his combs. Simply couldn't face'd. c.F.

* Fill in one week later

149

And, if Roald Dahl's suggestions, in *Matilda*, are anything to judge by, the school report can be such a lethal weapon that the schemes and scams for avoiding them plotted above might not be such a bad idea.

> School teachers suffer a good deal from having to listen to this sort of twaddle from proud parents, but they usually get their own back when the time comes to write the end-of-term reports. If I were a teacher I would cook up some real scorchers for the children of doting parents. 'Your son Maximilian,' I would write, 'is a total wash-out. I hope you have a family business you can push him into when he leaves school because he sure as heck won't get a job anywhere else.' Or if I were feeling lyrical that day, I might write, 'It is a curious truth that grasshoppers have their hearing-organs in the sides of the abdomen. Your daughter Vanessa, judging by what she's learnt this term, has no hearing-organs at all.'
>
> I might even delve deeper into natural history and say, 'The periodical cicada spends six years as a grub underground, and no more than six *days* as a free creature of sunlight and air. Your son Wilfred has spent six years as a grub in this school and we are still waiting for him to emerge from the chrysalis.' A particularly poisonous little girl might sting me into saying, 'Fiona has the same glacial beauty as an iceberg, but unlike an iceberg she has absolutely nothing below the surface.' I think I might enjoy writing end-of-term reports for the stinkers in my class.

And, not just to get your own back on the 'stinkers' . . . Though perhaps Miss Jean Brodie in her prime would not use so crude a tactic, her fellow teachers were not above expressing their hostility towards Miss

Brodie's free-thinking and unorthodox teaching methods through the school report.

> [Miss Gaunt, who] did not care at all for the Brodie set, who were
> stunned by a sudden plunge into industrious learning and very put out by
> Miss Gaunt's horrible sharpness and strict insistence on silence through-
> out the day . . . the black-marks book which eventually reflected itself on
> the end-of-term reports, was heavily scored with the names of the Brodie
> set by the end of the first week.

Perhaps the oddest 'report' is to be found in *Decline and Fall*. Evelyn
Waugh's Captain Grimes left school

> soon after my sixteenth birthday. But my house-master was a public
> school man. He knew the system.
>
> 'Grimes,' he said, 'I can't keep you in the House after what has hap-
> pened. I have the other boys to consider. But I don't want to be too hard
> on you. I want you to start again.'
>
> So he sat down there and then and wrote me a letter of recommenda-
> tion to any future employer, a corking good letter too. I've got it still. It's
> been very useful at one time or another. That's the public school system
> all over. They may kick you out, but they never let you down.

The Last Word

Laurie Lee (1914–97)

Writer

CENTRAL BOYS' SCHOOL, STROUD

Miss French, his English mistress, wrote of Lee, aged 15:

Off you go and I'm glad to get rid of you.

Acknowledgements

First and foremost I would like to thank the many people who sent me their reports. Such a good-natured response to what might have seemed an irritating request helped make compiling this book a great pleasure. Lots of others took the time to reply, even when their reports had long since vanished. I naively promised to try and track down reports from schools; to all those who gave me permission to use whatever I could unearth, I'm sorry to say that I came up with an almost total blank.

I am also very grateful to the many teachers, Heads and others who have spoken to me and furnished me with wonderful material: Nigel Richardson, Ian Thorpe, Ian Matheson, Margaret Chandler, Roger Lewis, Jennifer Warburton, Ann Hislop-Gill, Rebecca Treays, Sean Magee, Judith Hannam and Andrew Nickolds.

Thanks, too, to the Dyslexia Institute who have supported this book from the start.

Finally, thanks to Helen Gummer at Simon & Schuster for giving me the idea and to Katharine Young and Cassandra Campbell for seeing it through.

157

Sources

The following list gives in order of appearance in the book the sources of each entry with copyright details where appropriate. I have omitted all entries where the source is the subject. The editor and publishers are grateful to all the copyright holders for permission to reproduce material under their control. It has not proved possible to trace the copyright holder of every report, and we would be grateful to be notified of any corrections, which will be incorporated in reprints and future editions of this volume.

Nicholas Craig's report from *I, An Actor*, Christopher Douglas & Nigel Planer, Methuen, 2002 courtesy of the author; Peter Cook from *Peter Cook, A Biography*, Hodder & Stoughton Publishers, 1997 courtesy Radley College; Peter Ustinov's report from *Ustinov* by Christopher Warwick, Sidgwick & Jackson, 1990, courtesy the author; Alan Coren's report from *Could do Better* by Patrick Dickinson, Arrow, 1982; *David Lean* by Kevin Brownlow, Faber & Faber Ltd, 1997; Joan Collins' report from *Could do Better* by Patrick Dickinson, Arrow, 1982; John Lennon's report from *Shout* by Philip Norman, Elm Tree, Penguin Books, 1981 with permission Peters, Fraser & Dunlop; Norman Wisdom's report from *Could do Better* by Patrick Dickinson, Arrow, 1982; *Woody Allen* by John Baxter, Harper Collins, 1999; Beaverbrook's from *Beaverbrook* by A. J. P. Taylor, Penguin Books, 1974, with permission David Higham Associates; Sue Lawley's from *Could do Better* by Patrick Dickinson, Arrow, 1982; *A. A. Milne: His Life* by Ann Thwaite, Faber & Faber Ltd, 1990; *Augustus John* by Michael Holroyd, Chatto & Windus, 1996; *Wodehouse* by Frances Donaldson, Weidenfeld & Nicolson, 1982; Rupert Brooke - King's; *The Old Century and Seven Years More* by Siegfried Sassoon, Faber & Faber, 1938; *Cyril Connolly* by Jeremy Lewis, Jonathan Cape, 1997; *Cecil Beaton* by Hugo Vickers, Weidenfeld & Nicolson, 1985; *Graham Greene, Vol. II* by Norman Sherry, Jonathan Cape; *A Sort of Life*, Graham Greene, Simon & Schuster; *Dennis Potter* by Humphrey Carpenter, Faber & Faber Ltd, 1998; *Chatwin* by Nicholas Shakespeare, The Harvill Press, 1999; *H. H. Asquith* by Roy Jenkins, Collins; Churchill material from The Churchill Archive at Churchill College, Cambridge and with the permission of Curtis Brown and The Chartwell Trust; *Clement Attlee* by Kenneth Harris, Weidenfeld & Nicolson; *Stafford Cripps* by Chris Bryant, Hodder & Stoughton, 1997; *Anthony Eden* by Robert Rhodes James, Weidenfeld & Nicolson; *Alec Douglas-Home* by DR Thorpe, Sinclair-Stevenson, 1996; *One of Us* by Hugo Young, Macmillan, 1989; J. M. Keynes' material: Unpublished writings of M. Keynes, copyright The Provost and Scholars of King's College,

Cambridge, 2002, King's College Library, Cambridge; *Lord Longford* by Peter Stanford, Heinemann, 1994; F. D. R.'s report courtesy of the Franklin D. Roosevelt Library, Hyde Park, New York; *Eleanor Roosevelt* by Blance Wiesen Cook, Bloomsbury, 1993; Eisenhower's courtesy of the Eisenhower Library, Abilene, KS; J. F. K.'s courtesy of the John F. Kennedy Library, Boston, MA; Carter's courtesy of the Carter Library; George Bush Sr courtesy of The Bush Library; *A Life in the Twentieth Century* by Arthur M. Schlesinger, Jr, Houghton Miflin, 2000; Montgomery's from *Montgomery* by Nigel Hamilton and courtesy of St Paul's School; Mountbatten's from *Mountbatten* by Philip Ziegler, Collins, 1985 and with the permission of Emberdove Ltd; Heseltine's from *Heseltine* by Michael Crick, Penguin, 1996 and with the permission of Lord Heseltine; *Michael Foot* by Mervyn Jones, Gollancz, 1994; John Polanyi's courtesy Manchester Grammar; *The Secret Life of J Edgar Hoover* by Anthony Summers, Orion Publishing Group, 1993; Diana's from *Diana: Portrait of a Troubled Princess* by Sally Beddell Smith, Random House USA and quoted elsewhere; *The Heart has its Reasons* by Duchess of Windsor, Michael Joseph, 1956; *Carl Gustav Jung* by Frank McLynn, Bantam Press, used by permission of Transworld, a division of Random House Group Ltd; *Isaiah Berlin* by Michael Ignatieff, Chatto & Windus, 1999, courtesy St Paul's; *A. J. Ayer* by Ben Rogers, Chatto & Windus, 1999; *John Arlott* by Tim Arlott, Andre Deutsch, 1994; *Jennings Goes to School* by Anthony Buckeridge, Macmillan, 1996; *Billy Bunter at Greyfriars School* by Frank Richards, Hawk Books, Northants; *William and the School Report and Other Stories*, Richmal Crompton adapted by Martin Jarvis, Macmillan, 2000; *The Fib and Other Stories* by George Layton, Lion, 1981, 1988; *Molesworth, How to be Topp* by Geoffrey Willans and Ronald Searle, Penguin Classics, 2000 with permission Tessa Sayle Agency; *Matilda* by Roald Dahl with permission David Higham Associates; *The Prime of Miss Jean Brodie* by Muriel Spark, Penguin Classics; *Decline & Fall* by Evelyn Waugh, Penguin Classics.

The Dyslexia Institute

What is dyslexia?

Dyslexia causes difficulties in learning to read, write and spell. Short-term memory, mathematics, concentration, personal organisation and sequencing may also be affected.

Dyslexia usually arises from a weakness in the processing of language-based information. Biological in origin, it tends to run in families, but environmental factors also contribute.

Dyslexia can occur at any level of intellectual ability. It is not the result of poor motivation, emotional disturbance, sensory impairment or lack of opportunities, but it may occur alongside any of these.

The effects of dyslexia can be largely overcome by skilled specialist teaching and the use of compensatory strategies.

Dyslexia is the most common of the learning difficulties, affecting 10% of the UK population. Up to 4% has severe dyslexia, including some 375,000 schoolchildren. It can affect anyone of any age.

Dyslexia is complex due to variation in the number, type and severity of its associated difficulties. The manifestation of the difficulties dyslexia causes is influenced by the individual's personality and intelligence, parents, schooling and/or social and economic background. All these factors make dyslexia a very individual condition.

The Dyslexia Institute

Dyslexia can affect an individual's performance, have serious social implications and cause behavioural problems as a result of continuous underachievement. It is for this reason that the Dyslexia Institute (DI) is dedicated to ensuring that as many individuals with dyslexia are identified and helped as possible.

The DI is an educational charity, founded in 1972. It has grown to become the only national dyslexia teaching organisation in the world. The Institute carries out assessments for children and adults who may have dyslexia, provides specialist tuition for dyslexic people of all ages, trains specialist teachers, develops teaching materials and conducts research to ensure best provision and support for dyslexic people.

The DI employs over 220 specialist teachers, its own chartered psychologists, speech and language therapists, and support staff. In addition, some 70 educational psychologists work for the DI on a consultancy basis. The Institute has 26 main Centres and over 140 smaller teaching units throughout the country but it is continuously working to increase its outreach.

This year the Institute celebrates 30 years of best practice. Its continued mission is to see all dyslexic people identified and taught so that they are able to reach their full potential and make the maximum contribution to society.

Could Do Better

"Could do better", is a term that some individuals who are dyslexic will remember from their school days. However, many dyslexic people are often artistic, creative, original, lateral thinkers and as a result very often excel in careers such as design, engineering, architecture, IT or medicine. There are many dyslexic individuals who do very well in their chosen professions but the DI strives to ensure that all people with dyslexia have an equal opportunity to reach their full potential.

The Dyslexia Institute is dependent upon fees from assessments, teaching and training courses, income from the sale of publications, fundraising and the generosity of benefactors. It would like to thank Simon & Schuster and Catherine Hurley on behalf of all dyslexic people for supporting it in raising awareness of dyslexia.

For More Information:

Address: The Dyslexia Institute, Park House, Wick Road,
Egham, Surrey, TW20 0HR
Tel: 01784 222300
E-Mail: info@dyslexia-inst.org.uk

Please visit the DI's website at www.dyslexia-inst.org.uk

Catherine Hurley is a freelance editor and writer. Her school reports in Canada suggested she could do better by moving to England. After ten years' working in publishing she decided she could do better bringing up her two children.